THE ENGLISHMAN'S ROOM

·

EDITED BY
ALVILDE LEES-MILNE

·

PHOTOGRAPHS BY
DERRY MOORE

VIKING

VIKING

Penguin Books Ltd, Harmondsworth, Middlesex, England
Viking Penguin Inc., 40 West 23rd Street, New York, New York
10010, U.S.A.
Penguin Books Australia Ltd, Ringwood, Victoria, Australia
Penguin Books Canada Limited, 2801 John Street, Markham,
Ontario, Canada L3R 1B4
Penguin Books (N.Z.) Ltd, 182–190 Wairau Road, Auckland 10,
New Zealand

First published 1986

Designed by Paul Bowden

Typeset in Aldus by
Rowland Phototypesetting Limited
Bury St Edmunds, Suffolk
Printed in Italy

British Library Cataloguing in Publication Data
Lees-Milne, Alvilde
The Englishman's room.
1. Interior decoration
I. Title
747.7′5   NK2117.L5
ISBN 0-670-80791-5

Previous page James Lees-Milne in his library

CONTENTS

PREFACE

Here we have a group of intelligent men, all of them in their several ways creative. They consist of well-known politicians, painters, actors, art historians, decorators, owners of historic houses, and writers. What unites them is that all have homes of their own to which they are deeply attached, and in these homes, large or small, there is one room which means more to them than any other. In fact it means a very great deal. These men may frequently be away from home, travelling round the world, delivering speeches, sitting on immensely important committees on which our fate depends, acting on the stage literally or metaphorically, carrying out their duties, being in the public eye, or endeavouring to keep out of the public eye. Whatever they may be doing at home or abroad they will consciously or unconsciously have at the back of their minds one special room to which they long to return. For this room is singularly precious to them. It may be filled with objects collected or inherited over the years – rich and rare treasures, or mere souvenirs like old walking-sticks and sea-shells. In this room their whole personality is enshrined.

Few people in the Western world are nomadic. Most civilized human beings share with animals the need for a nest or lair in which they may seek protection from the bustling world outside – sometimes inside – and relax. What is fascinating is the different way in which men regard and treat their special room. To some it is a holy sanctum to which no one is admitted. Not even a wife is encouraged to inspect the torn cushion covers, far less to disturb the piles of last year's *Country Life* or *Sporting News*. To others it is a communal meeting place where family and guests are welcomed with open arms and children encouraged to litter the floor and sofas with plastic toys. Only in such surroundings was Anthony Trollope able to compose the Barchester novels. For Quentin Bell his favourite room is literally a workshop of tools and revolving wheels in which he makes his pottery. For Sir John Gielgud his (actually not in his house) is a theatre dressing-room where among the pots of make-up he nostalgically looks back over a long and glamorous stage career. For Nigel Nicolson his is yet another kind of workshop unadorned by anything but dictionaries and filing cabinets.

Some writers like to sit with their back to the window to avoid distraction from outside. Others prefer to face the garden, if they have one, in order to be distracted. Some of those who live in a town find in the noise and roar of traffic a communion with humanity without which they would feel isolated and lonely. One of the contributors, having been brought up in one of the grandest houses of England, has his retreat in the smallest room available for reasons which are as amusing as they are understandable.

There are those men who like clutter and those who prefer emptiness and order. Those who prefer the insignificant and those the aesthetic. Those who like the splendid and even those who seemingly relish the squalid. A remarkable difference between the sexes is that nearly every woman's favourite room is the bedroom – among our thirty men contributors only two choose their bedroom as their favourite room.

In Victorian times the paterfamilias's 'study' – a word incidentally eschewed today by at least two contributors – was often a terrifying place to servants and children. To be summoned to the 'study', with its masculine odour of cigar smoke and macassar oil, almost certainly portended in the one case dismissal, and in the other punishment. In both it engendered fear and trembling. Today 'Dad's den', if it exists at all, is a more benign substitute because the barriers between the generations are now down.

Possessions and decoration play a large part in the rooms these men have chosen to write about, and they are immensely varied in size, content and environment, ranging as they do over England, France, Italy, Greece and America.

ALVILDE LEES-MILNE

SIR HAROLD ACTON

ITALY

Though an Englishman living in Italy, where I was born, I'm afraid that my choice of a favourite room is not typically English. Perhaps the mixture of furniture and bric-à-brac is more English than Italian, for Italians tend to live more out of doors than my compatriots, and their rooms are either on parade – 'per far figura' – or bleakly functional.

In the last eighty years I have slept in more bedrooms than I can remember. Some had blue views of hills and green views of gardens; others were visited by birds and squirrels – the ragamuffin crows of Calcutta alighted on my breakfast table and flew off with a slice of papaya; the inquisitive squirrels of Berkeley, California, were scarcely less shy at my window-sill. The fleeting visits of these creatures helped me to confront the day's business in an optimistic mood, though the rooms in themselves might lack any memorable feature. The most featureless allowed me to write fluently, for they contained nothing to distract the mind, which is an advantage for a writer.

Paradoxically, the bedroom I prefer is full of distractions. In a fifteenth-century house this is the only eighteenth-century apartment, divided by a stuccoed arch with a delicate chandelier whose crystal drops glitter like prismatic diamonds on the dullest of days.

My bed lies between four rococo posts, carved and gilded, and it is broad enough to accommodate a strenuous couple. As far as I know it only accommodates myself. The mattress is solid: I dislike plushy couches that smother one. (I will spare the reader an account of my dreams – usually a collage of the people I have known and books I have read.) A pile of volumes stands on the table beside it to beguile the dread hours of insomnia.

Through a high French window opposite, over a stone balcony facing south, I am stimulated by a statue of Bacchus astride a leopard flanked by nymphs bearing cornucopia under a triumphal arch of Tuscan *pietra serena*. Punctually every year hoopoes arrive

to nest on the urns above it. Their voices are soothing, if monotonous; their crests are superb. Clumps of ilex in the background conceal the distant hills. A rusticated wall behind them separates the garden from a farm adjoining a convent, so that there is a pastoral symphony of crowing cocks, cackling hens, cooing pigeons and grunting pigs, alternating with chapel bells at regular intervals. In June the coloratura of nightingales drowns the hooting of owls and the croaking of frogs. All this is outside the room: I need no radio.

The cream-coloured walls are covered with paintings. The most English of these are views of Venice, not by Canaletto, alas, but by a later Venetian, Giuseppe Borsato: bull-baiting outside the Doge's palace and the square of St Mark. Almost as English are two landscapes by Zuccarelli, but the Madonna and Child by Francesco de Mura is typically Neapolitan, and the portraits of eighteenth-century ladies are provincial Italian, sweetly pretty except for Queen Maria Carolina of Naples, who was plainer than her sister Marie Antoinette but more intelligent. It is due to her that my ancestors settled in Naples. A black-lacquered cabinet and chest of drawers contains a few Far Eastern associations, little bronze Buddhas, Chinese snuff-bottles, and an ivory seal of the Ming dynasty carved with a brooding cat. On a bureau of walnut wood a row of medals of the last Medici in profile and a bronze bust of Ferdinand I and IV of the Two Sicilies remind me of the books I have written and the pleasures I owe them. The overhanging mirror could not be described in U-language as a looking-glass, for its mottled verdigris surface is too sombre for reflection: its grace is concentrated in the curvaceous frame of dusty gold.

I confess I prefer most vases to the cut flowers that fill them, especially if they are of Chinese porcelain, but a selection of blooms is welcome with the change of season.

A cluster of Venetian glass fruit on a scagliola-topped guéridon is diversified with sea-shells inter-

Above The stuccoed arch separating the bed from
the rest of the room.
Right The bed with its four carved and gilded posts.

twined with a Tibetan rosary of tiny carved skulls –
memento mori. An Eton-blue escritoire . . . But
hold! 'Are you compiling an inventory?' the reader
will complain. Yet this inventory evokes my bedroom, whose contents are precious to me even if they
would not 'fetch' – I believe that is the term – a record
sum in a London sale-room.

I suppose this assortment of objects does reflect my
personality. Perhaps I am too attached to my possessions. Having lost a houseful of valued objects in
Peking during the last world war, I should have
reached a spiritual state of non-attachment, but now
it is too late. I cling to those that remain. Obviously it
would be difficult to re-create such a room elsewhere,
for its outlook on a Tuscan garden is essential to its

atmosphere. I would not care to live in a room,
however luxurious, arranged by an interior decorator. The 'good taste' of the most successful decorator
is too impersonal for mine. I go so far as to prefer the
countrified Italian furniture of the eighteenth century to the polished, impeccable products of Louis
Quinze. In hotel rooms I suffer from a creeping
malaise, yet I am reluctant to inflict myself on friends
abroad with a single exception. I leave the gentle
reader to guess. She can create a special climate with a
few cushions, a little needlework, and a footstool. She
alone can revive cut flowers so that they almost
confide in one while they intoxicate with their fra-
grance.

HARDY AMIES

OXFORDSHIRE

The pleasure of building is denied to all but the very rich. Magnates with taste are as rare as are the unselfish. Furthermore, even fervid home-builders have their enthusiasm and invention dampened, if not extinguished, by a multitude of regulations, controlled by local councils and executed by councillors and their servants of little knowledge and less taste.

Today is the day of the conversion: rectories, mills, oasthouses, stables, chapels and of course barns: all tempt the would-be home-maker.

I am a Cancerian. I am a home-maker. My main dwelling is a village schoolhouse built in 1840. The schoolroom makes a comfortable and fairly large living-room; but there is only one, and there is only one guest room. The size of the garden is determined firmly by the stone walls of the former playground, mercifully un-asphalted. I suffer as do all village small-holders from a lack of space.

After a few years' residence, when the pleasures of achievement were wearing thin and drawbacks came to the surface, a chance to buy a barn with a tennis court, a courtyard and some surrounding plots suitable for flower-beds proved irresistible. The plot had been at one time a farmyard, was stone-wall enclosed and was two minutes' walk from the schoolhouse.

The tennis court was used immediately. The barn became the family garage. The walls were of stone and the roof, recently repaired, was of reconstituted Cotswold tiles. There were tall openings on the north and south where barn doors had been. It was a sturdy shell.

I soon realized that it had a marvellous position. My village, on the fringe of the Cotswolds, is in flat and often windswept country. The façade of barn facing the tennis court was due south and very protected. Even the north side had a courtyard and then houses in front of it. I soon made flower-beds – mostly old-fashioned roses, which would be unsightly in the non-flowering months in the small formal garden at the schoolhouse. It was pleasant to

The Barn room detached from the house is used for various forms of entertainment.

12

sit out after tennis with the barn walls behind you and the sun in front, which shone all day over the fields stretching away to the Thames and the Berkshire hills.

I fell, of course. First came a much deserved greenhouse in the south corner of the courtyard. Then the barn itself was tackled.

It was easy to make a large fireplace on the centre of the north side. We just filled in the opening. Exactly opposite, on the south, came French windows, flanked by further windows, with deep recesses. The beams were in perfect condition, except for the swallows' and martins' visiting cards which I preserved carefully.

What did I have the room for? Firstly as a super-pavilion for tennis. So there were built two bathrooms, one with a shower, like a changing room. Then there is a small room for kitchen sink and refrigerator, and electric kettle and tiny stove for modest meals.

Secondly I wanted a room for parties. At the west end I built an indoor barbecue with glazed tiles and a chimney. This is not wholly successful as the chimney smokes. (Unlike the main fireplace which draws like a giant inhaling marijuana.)

The room of course works beautifully for summer parties. The French windows open on to a gravelled plot, box-edged, where live four lemon trees in tubs. It also performs its duties in the winter, especially at Christmas time.

Thirdly it is a room for guests to escape to or to be escaped from. Upstairs there are two bedrooms. So it is a guest house.

Fourthly it is a music room: the acoustics are very good. If this sounds grand, I really only use it to study opera with libretto, before going to a festival like Salzburg or Glyndebourne. There is no telephone.

Fifthly it is a feast room. There is room for a round table (dismantled when not in use) for ten people. These are fed usually from the barbecue with locally made sausages. Smoke problems are solved by using small Japanese charcoal burners. I use cardboard plates which get burnt ceremoniously on the log fire.

It was the idea of having a feast room which inspired me originally to do the conversion. Some of my early purchases for the room were the pine refectory table, seen here used as a sofa table, and lots of kitchen chairs. To these have now been added the oak seventeenth-century armchairs of which I am particularly fond and which are remarkably comfortable for conversation. It was only after a year or two that becoming tired of guests' complaints of my austerity I fell for a Howard sofa and two armchairs, bought from that ever constant supplier, Frank Williams in Burford. I have always had help from Colefax and Fowler for any successful room. Tom Parr advised their Tree Paeony chintz, with which I couldn't be happier.

A sixth role the room has to play is that of a library: for bound volumes of *Punch* (only to 1930) and of *Country Life*; for books on travel, on music and on art. For these I had made by a local carpenter the breakfront bookcase in oak. When I found I needed more space I ordered two more bookcases to flank the fireplace. Workhouse fever made me choose pine instead of oak, which I forever regret. When will we ever learn?

The plastered walls are washed with cream distemper. The curtains are of heavy cream cotton. The window recesses are lined with blue and white tiles, as is the barbecue.

Visitors always ask about the large plates on the bookcase. These came from the Conran shop in Sloane Avenue and were the work of a talented protégé of Terence Conran's sister. The jumbo-sized drug jars on the fireplace came from a shop in the square at Orvieto.

I don't mind if the stag heads look pretentious. There is every reason to believe they once belonged to the Winter Queen, my favourite lady in history. There are similar trophies at Ashdown House, built by Lord Craven, the Queen's protector, and now owned by the National Trust, who bought the stag heads. So they must have confidence in them.

I love my possessions like the oak armchairs; but I now begin to make lists, sometimes only in my mind, of the objects I shall leave to friends when I am dead.

The room at the barn gives me immense pleasure. Its proportions are right: it houses old furniture, books and means of making music. It is an ante-room to the tennis court and garden. It's a place to lodge, and to give cheer to friends.

The three stag's heads above the fireplace may have belonged
to the Queen of Bohemia.

QUENTIN BELL

SUSSEX

Artists who work with their hands need a place which can stand harsh treatment – a studio, or, if the treatment be very harsh – a workshop.

The studio in its most florid incarnation is a theatre not only of labour but of display, almost a drawing-room. There are still a few such palatial abodes of art in London, and I suppose, elsewhere; but for an easily accessible source showing us the studio in all its glory, we need look no further than the pages of *Punch* in the days of Du Maurier. Here we may find a quite wonderful confection of gold and velvet, crystal, mahogany and heaven knows what else. The model's throne is indeed imperial, and here the duchess may be immortalized in her natural surroundings. That the more sublime genre may be pursued, a boy in buttons, a handsome boy with unfashionably long hair, will, when unbuttoned, impersonate Ganymede or Patroclus. Coexisting with this kind of studio there is another. It is an attic, with a broken skylight, an empty stove and an emaciated young man, perhaps a genius. The attic persists in one form or another, but the palace of art is out of fashion. In our country there is a tendency to feel that the studio should be a workshop, and pretty plain. Although its austerity may be relieved by laminated wood and expensive-looking metal, it keeps a businesslike air. I think that the most businesslike studio I have seen was a Parisian room, handsome but bare. It had, I believe, served an embassy from Savoy in the seventeenth century. In 1937 it was devoted to the production of one picture: 'Guernica'. It did not entirely serve that purpose, for the canvas was so large that it had to be set askew at one end of the room. For the rest, there was a table covered with great cans of decorators' paint, three kitchen chairs, and on the floor a vast array of tins and jars each containing a different mixture of colours. To me it was a miracle that the artist did not send a dozen of these paint-pots flying as he moved to and fro in front of his picture.

That was indeed a workshop used simply for the production of one great picture.

The studios that I knew in my youth were a compromise. They had nothing of the salon about them but clearly were intended not only for working but for living. This, especially when the occupant is a woman, makes for a more civilized environment. There are sofas and curtains, paintings, and decorations on the walls. Here no effort was made to attain the austere aesthetic neutrality of the workshop. The place was itself a work of art and one could easily tell what kind of painting would be brought out of it. That particular genre is a thing of the past. So far as I know only one example survives – the newly repaired and restored studio at Charlston Farm House.

I have lived and worked in a number of studios, including a scene-painter's studio in the Via Magutta. This was so high that by candlelight I could not see the ceiling. It was the coldest place in Rome that winter. I lived in one corner of it, and there was always far more space than one could use. But I have been much more concerned with workshops adapted for the ceramic arts and here, almost always, one is looking for space. Civilized life is practically impossible; all one's arrangements are dominated by three essential engines of the craft: the big high wedging table, the throwing wheel and the kiln (unless it be set outside the pottery). A pottery must have these three major items of equipment, but one needs other things: colours, stains, glazes, oxides, kiln furniture, brushes, lining wheels, sponges, steel tools, wire tools, boxwood tools, wire, sieves, innumerable space-filling moulds, and hundreds of other things. So one must have shelves, and then more shelves, and cupboards, and then there must be water and ways of disposing of the water when it has turned to liquid clay and will block the pipes, and airtight bins and plastic bags; and still more shelves . . . Only once have I for a time had all the room I needed, and even then I overflowed my proper banks so that when I

moved to more restricted quarters there was a crisis.

The potter then must think in terms of space and action, for he must have room to move himself and his wares and impedimenta from place to place, and somewhere to settle comfortably to work with all his gear around him. Unlike the painter he is not much worried by problems of light. He may arrange for an enjoyable view on every side, and needs much artificial light and many 15-amp plugs.

The artists of the Quattrocento lived above their workshops and in this showed their wisdom, as one may reflect when, having remembered at midnight that one has failed to throw a switch on the kiln, one slips on a dressing-gown and makes one's way over a snow-covered yard to the pottery, only to discover that one's memory has played one false. Today, thank heavens, I can walk out of my sitting-room into my workshop. But now the trouble is, so far as the rest of the household is concerned, that I can walk back again, and that in so doing I can leave a clear record of my progress across tiles, floorboards, carpets upstairs and downstairs, in that gluey mixture of glaze, plaster, mud and clay which strikes so discordant a note in a well-kept home. One needs some kind of *cordon sanitaire*, something perhaps like those tin foot-baths which are provided for the purification of men and beasts on a farm menaced by foot-and-mouth disease, anything that will keep the rich detritus of the pottery from invading the rest of the house. I suppose that a more lively conscience on the part of the potter is the true answer.

It should be borne in mind that the invaders may come from without. Most potters will have memories of kind, well-meaning visitors, children perhaps, who, exclaiming 'Oh, how lovely!', take a plate by the rim and lift it off a shelf, or at least try to do so, not realizing that at this stage of its life clay can be as brittle and friable as shortcake, so that the well-meaning stranger is left with a fraction of the plate between his fingers while the rest remains where it was, looking half eaten. For all that it is not easy to deny entrance to such visitors, because there is an element of magic in ceramic work far exceeding that which from early youth we experience in the making of mud pies – not that mud pies should be underestimated. The solid lump of clay upon the wheel, rough, irregular and amorphous, which is suddenly yet smoothly compelled to rise in a column and then sink into itself once more, to rise as a vase or a bowl or a plate, is surely almost as much of a treat for the spectator as it is for the thrower. The band drawn with a motionless brush upon a revolving dish, the splash of vivid colour, the sharp calligraphic effect made by a sharp tool cutting through white clay, all these and a hundred other technical feats can be a delight to watch even when the artist is not outstandingly skilful or talented. There are other delights, the unpacking from the furnace of wares metamorphosed by great heat and all the possibilities of joy or disappointment over disasters and fortunate accidents. These belong rather to a later stage of production. But perhaps the visitor may see enough to learn that the potter's workshop is a place of the happiest industry and that it is inhabited by very fortunate people.

Previous page The potter's workshop, with some
of the many tools needed.
Right A handsome plate and some craftsman's tools.

SIMON BLOW

LONDON

My home is a two-roomed flat situated on the first floor of an eighteenth-century London house. For me, it is a place to work, sleep, and sometimes entertain. But because writing is a solitary occupation I find it necessary to live somewhere that has its individual imprint. For instance, I do not think I would be happy in a room that was an empty space – a style of living that I know can be so fashionable. My flat is more of a natural home, filled with different associations from my life. In that way I am able to wander and dream from present to past, and risk an occasional glimpse at the future.

A pair of double doors partitions the room where I write and sleep, and the room where I entertain. From my desk I look out to a clinical modern building that is at odds with the eighteenth-century panelling of my bedroom's interior. But I don't mind the contrast, for it would surely be a mistake to live oblivious to the moods of our time. And anyway, within the flat there are plenty of escape routes for an imagination blistered by the contemporary landscape. There are my books; my paintings; and those little objects of sentiment that I find I am always picking up and putting down. Enough, in fact, to distract one from the limitations of here and now.

I think it was Huysmans's delicate hero of *À Rebours* who claimed that really one could see the world so much better from one's armchair, and I like where I live to provide this stimulant. In my sitting-room I have two pen-and-ink watercolours by my great-uncle Stephen Tennant. They are boulevard scenes of Marseilles, evoking the shady glamour of the old quarter. The paintings are crowded with smirking matelots, pouting cocottes, lascars and vagrants. Stray items are worked on to the page, such as an opened packet of cigarettes named *Trois Cœurs*, lists of maritime arrivals and departures, and a fortune-teller's card promising to 'Ramène affection' (re-unite loved ones). I have never been to Marseil-

les, and I feel like Huysmans's hero Des Esseintes. He cancels a visit to England, certain in his imagination that he has already been there. Living with Uncle Stephen's adventurous boulevards, I too am certain that I have been to Marseilles.

Sentimentality is often confused with sentiment; I have never cared much for the former but I have no embarrassment about indulging the latter. The many personal things that I surround myself with are links with childhood or family that I want to preserve. Next to where I write is a watercolour by my father of a wonderful English Renaissance portico belonging to a house where I played as a child. The house was a ruin on my great-aunt's estate in Leicestershire, and we used to run through its crumbling, empty passages making up stories about the people who had lived there. Above it is a portrait of my mother by the society photographer Bassano, a reminder of how she looked while I was growing up. And in my sitting-room I tend to cluster my memories along the mantelpiece. Two Jacobean-style dolls that I have known all my life. They were given to my father at his birth by his godfather, Lord Kitchener. (My grandfather, the architect Detmar Blow, had designed a house for Kitchener, and was a friend of his.) Then there are the photographs from childhood, which I shuffle and rearrange from time to time. I value the disturbance that these pictures bring: the return of vanished worlds made more vivid by their poignancy.

Perhaps I have unconsciously created for myself an atmosphere that brings back that line from A. E. Housman: 'Into my heart an air that kills from yon far country blows.' I say unconsciously because I have always looked back, ever since I was a child – for me it is a natural condition. Maybe too I have given my rooms the cosiness of certain rooms that I knew and loved in childhood, but altered of course by the imprint of my own personality. But the flat's character does not seem easy for others to gauge. Some say it is an apartment in Paris, or, with its front windows

Books unite the two rooms, making them seem like one.

The dark-blue walls are densely covered
with prints, drawings and gouaches.

brushed by a low tree and facing a building that is 1930s 'modern', one in New York. Then I have been told it is like two rooms chopped off from some larger house in the country. Although it sits in an eighteenth-century town house, with a part eighteenth-century interior, it is rarely identified with London. Possibly I should be pleased that my place of being has escaped labels.

I do not think I could be described as a social person; at least not in conventional terms. For instance, I dislike a diary that is filled with dinner invitations. Once or twice a fortnight is quite enough. Talking to people can be very tiring and frequently, alas, a disappointment. I do enjoy entertaining here, but I like to do so on an impromptu basis. Seeing people is far more relaxing if you have

friends who do not mind being asked over at the last minute. And for dinners my flat is really best suited to four; but I am often at my happiest with one or two.

Running through both rooms are my books. Because I am always going to my library, they unite the two rooms and make me think of them as one. I use my books constantly for work and pleasure. They are a living part of my life to me, and I have often been puzzled by houses where books exist simply for decoration. In these houses it is not unusual to find the people a little dead, like the books. This malaise particularly affects sections of the English upper class, and I must first have begun to read seriously as an outlet from this claustrophobia. I remember how I used to feel guilt at reading in houses where Milton

The mantelpiece holds a nice
cluster of memorabilia.

and Shakespeare were as foreign as gondolas. To read throughout an afternoon was considered a strange idleness; if caught I would shift uncomfortably in my chair. Now this guilt has long since gone, and defying those philistine frowns I will often read for a day on my bed, propped up by pillows.

Occupying all of my space, I need not be haunted by the fear that obsessed the melancholic Sir George Sitwell at his Derbyshire seat, Renishaw. He would be heard to mutter that wherever he was in his house, he was sure there was always the sound of laughter in the next room. But the advantage of a compact place is that it lies ready to entertain just one. Thus the shock of possible solitude is lessened. And while such a life would not be suitable for those who depend on the tittle-tattle as witnessed by Saint-Simon, for those of another disposition the peace that can be found in a single space is very welcoming.

So I suppose that for me I have made my flat my refuge. Apart from the many personal mementoes, I have furnished it in a way that keeps the horrors of our world at bay. But this is not escapism; it is the necessity for calm. Home, after all, is where we should draw our strength. Though as life goes on, it is increasingly the place where we recuperate. In the happenings of the larger world beyond there seems to be a delight in distress and uncertainty which I cannot share. Protection among the things that I know and love has become required security. And this is why I like to keep my own surroundings well in sight. In my room, which is my home, I know that I have at least been able to do that.

DIRK BOGARDE

FRANCE

The house was built as a shepherd's house in 1641 and added to in three sections as the family, and their fortunes, grew. When I first saw it sixteen years ago it was a solid, uncompromising, stone-built house under a long tiled roof, three storeys high, sitting fair and square to the winds on an abandoned terraced hillside.

The first floor sat directly on the earth without damp course or foundations; it still has neither and seems none the worse for that. When a boulder was discovered which was too big to be moved it was merely incorporated into the walls, all of which are at least a metre thick; perhaps these act as a sort of anchor?

The stout oak door opened directly into the kitchen (the earliest part of the house), which had an immense open fireplace with a canopy and a hand-hewn stone sink in one corner. Through a rough wooden door one went down two steps into an adjoining cow-stall which had held eight beasts and a rusty manger; next to that another plank door led down four steps into a cart-shed in which a battered Citroën car sat in the dust. All the floors were thus on different levels, but all the ceilings were uniform, supported by giant oak beams, heavily stained black.

The kitchen wall was roughly washed in thick khaki distemper, the cow-stall was built of uncut field stones and so was the cart-shed; cobwebs and dust were everywhere. In the kitchen the floor was covered with octagonal honey-coloured tiles, the cow-stall with cracked concrete, the cart-shed with old bricks laid directly on to the earth. They are still there to this day.

When I stood in the cart-shed and looked up through the two doorways towards the kitchen area, I knew that I had the basis for my longed-for, all white long-room. It would be at least twenty feet wide by fifty feet long, once a little architectural work had been done. This was entrusted to my brave architect, M. Leon Loschetter, who understood exactly what

I wanted and was very relieved that I did not wish acres of white wrought-iron, plate-glass, and parquet flooring, or swimming pools.

I insisted that the character of the house, both inside and out, must be retained at all costs, and that only the most ancient materials should be used in the reconstruction which we would have to make. We would open up the three rooms into one, by cutting wide arches in the thick walls, off-set so that the disagreeable effect of sitting in a tunnel would be avoided: the room must be one unit, but with three distinct sitting areas linked together by the massive beams above and the tiled floors below, from kitchen to cart-shed. The kitchen would remain intact, canopy, fireplace, stone sink and all; the great cart-shed doors were to become a window and a door combined, and the sagging door of the cow-stall, giving directly on to the land, would also become a window with a deep window-seat.

All windows faced south and must catch every scrap of light, winter and summer; the hideous black-stained beams were stripped down, sanded roughly, and then rag-washed with white. Walls were all plastered with an uneven surface and a coarse-textured finish, as in all old houses which have been built by peasant hands. The floors, except for the kitchen, and the cart-shed bricks, would be laid with ancient tiles removed from a demolished farm in the valley. The kitchen, with its canopied fireplace, was to be the focal centre of the room.

Work started in early April and was, amazingly, finished in July while I was away abroad working, all for the modest sum of £3,000. The finished, empty room when I first saw it that July was exactly as I had hoped and planned it to be, so much so that I almost resented the furniture and the chairs and sofas, in their frilly English chintzes, when they arrived to be unloaded, because they completely broke the white simplicity and perfect proportions. The chairs and the sofas were re-covered in a thick white woven cotton *instantly*. Almost! And everything brought over from England fitted in perfectly. This had all been planned (on graph-paper) months before, so each piece went to its designated position with ease.

So did all the paintings which, while not of great value, are ones which I have collected over the years and with which I have lived very happily always. These were never bought for 'value': merely for the pleasure of their company. If the canopy in the kitchen is one focal point (perhaps *the* focal point), then at the other end of the room, the cart-shed, Leonard Rosoman's 'The Wave' is the other.

The room is a sitting-room: that is to say, it is a room where people can sit, sprawl, read books, make conversation, listen to music, argue, knit, or relax in whatever way they wish. The paintings in this room are all modern: Joan Eardly, Christopher Wood, Rosoman, a Ben Nicholson which I particularly enjoy, two Mohnerets and a Picasso lithograph. They look, on the white walls with space all round them, like windows opening out to fantastic landscapes. It is a 'summer room' all the year round, for even in the depths of winter when the vine is bare, the wind howls and the snow drifts, the white walls and white covered chairs and sofas, the pictures and the bowls of flowers on every surface, reflect every gleam of light giving it clarity, warmth and the illusion of sunshine.

White is perhaps not the best colour for a room on a terraced hillside high up on the side of a modest mountain, with dogs carting mud about on broad feet, and guests wandering in from exhausting efforts with fork and trowel in the '*potager*', but, strangely, it seems to work perfectly well. The only thing that I really dread is a child with a chocolate biscuit, or one which is, as they often are at very tender ages, incontinent. I have had both, alas! But all that is the risk one has to take if one insists on a white room better suited, perhaps, to Beverly Hills or Grosvenor Square.

But this room is essentially designed to be lived in with ease and comfort, without restrictions. It is a perfectly simple room for a simple life-style. And as such I think, personally, that it works. I have no idea if it reflects my personality: how could I? But I do know that it has strong echoes of almost every room of its kind which I have owned in larger houses in England, and it contains all the same old bits and pieces, mostly gathered from junk shops, so that I am familiar with them and the room feels 'right' for me. Nothing here is new, and there is not a single stick of Louis-Anything, Boulle or Sèvres; which delights my French guests who sink into fat old armchairs with little cries of relieved comfort. It is considered '*très anglais*', although it is really a mix of all kinds of pieces.

I don't believe much in possessions as such: they are a tremendous tie and a liability and I have always thought that one suitcase would be enough for me.

However, if one puts down roots, even for a short amount of time, it is essential to be surrounded with things which give one pleasure and are comfortable and comforting at the same time. So possessions I am forced to have. If all that I presently own were to be destroyed suddenly I really don't think that I would grieve very much, save for the loss, perhaps, of the pictures, which have been a constant source of pleasure and which are irreplaceable.

There is no sign of a decorator's hand here either, which might be a good or a bad thing, depending on how one views the result. Obviously I have made furnishing 'errors' here and there, mixing style and period as I see fit and with what is to hand, but everything seems to be harmonious and nothing seems 'arranged'. There are no curtains (shutters do very well), no carpets, except a rush mat before the fire in winter, no tassels or pom-poms: just clear and simple lines and the pleasing glow of the tiled floor polished to a high degree. (Three coats of turpentine and linseed, half and half, rubbed into the floor and left to soak in for twenty-four hours, then buffed up with beeswax. An extremely exhausting, nail-breaking, knuckle-grazing job: but well worth it.)

The test of a room such as this is simple. Clearly it will, and it does, hold fifty or more people with ease, but what is it like with, say, only two or three? Do we rattle about like peas in a whistle? The answer is easy. It is still a place of harmony and comfort, a welcoming room, intimate and warm: a sitting-room as snug as a nursery, and as such it passes the test, in my opinion anyway.

Previous page Two of the wide arches that were cut in the thick walls to make one large room out of three. *Above* Another view of the room with spacious areas cleverly linked together.

RICHARD BUCKLE

DORSET

Although I was born in a cottage in Westmorland, and brought up in another in Norfolk, I don't think I ever had any ambition to *own* one. When I got out of the army in 1945, I am sure I expected to live in London for ever. Yet, come to think of it, during manoeuvres on Salisbury Plain in winter 1942–3, as I reeled like King Lear over the summits of the drenching downs, the idea did sometimes occur to me of how cosy it might be, if I survived, to inhabit one of those sheltered valleys of Avon, Wylye or Nadder down below, and drink wine beside a blazing fire; and that is what has happened.

It was Diaghilev who directed me back to Wiltshire, for in 1954, when I was organizing an exhibition to mark the twenty-fifth anniversary of his death, I made friends with his great supporter Lady Juliet Duff, and began to spend weekends with her at Bulbridge House, Wilton. Nine years later, exhausted by the preparations for another exhibition to celebrate Shakespeare's 400th birthday, I rented a cottage near Juliet at Broad Chalke so as to escape for two nights a week from the horde of artists, scholars, stage designers, musicians and scene-builders who were milling around my flat. In 1965 Landlady A. wanted her cottage back and I found my present home in a deep hollow eight miles away. Juliet, who had died that year, always said, 'Never live with a view!' Well, I don't.

All my friends thought this hovel too appalling, but perhaps it was my sordid vocation to make sow's ears into silk purses.

No, I don't really like cottages, but at least mine is not thatched. What is more, I can see the woods of Beckford's Fonthill from an eminence in my garden. I live a hermit's life, like Beckford, but with fewer servants. With none in fact.

Looking from the library
out into the garden.

I suppose my triple ground-floor room is what American architects would call an Open-Plan Living Area. (I do so hope the Dying Area will be my long attic bedroom upstairs.) It is not at all my ideal room. Nor were my previous Living Areas. From 1948 to 1955 I had a big underground drawing-room in Chelsea with Curzon Street-Baroque *boiseries*, huge Venetian paintings by Pittoni, Ricci and Pellegrini, flogged long since, and no windows except a skylight. I painted it crimson and white with a turquoise ceiling. Coming down the steps, Augustus John said, 'It's like the Arabian Nights.' Then for twenty-one years I dwelt above a Victorian bank overlooking old Covent Garden Market – noisy but central. The drawing-room was hung with grey moiré cotton-pretending-to-be-silk. These Wiltshire walls are whitewashed. Of course I should prefer high perfectly proportioned rooms and Louis Seize furniture. Who wouldn't? But it is a question not only of what one can afford, but also of what is appropriate to the locality. 'Consult the Genius of the Place in all.' I never stop quoting that or of bragging that Pope wrote it to my ancestor Burlington. The one thing which is exactly as I should wish it in my latest Living Area is that there are lots of books. Yet the disadvantage of this low-ceilinged cottage is that if you need more room for books you have to build on a wing. (I have had to give up taking in *Country Life* and *The World of Interiors* because I am too mean to throw my copies away.) The chief advantage is that I am remote and quiet, but only two hours from London when Maggie Smith is playing Millamant in *The Way of the World*.

So three rooms lead out of each other. Let us call them the dining-room, the library and the sitting-room. The first is part of the old labourer's cottage, built of green sandstone in the eighteenth or even the seventeenth century, probably by blind-drunk peasants at midnight and certainly before news of the right angle had reached this corner of the county. The three-foot-thick walls lean and bulge like the décor of a UFA film. Did those rude forefathers of the hamlet know they were working on the site of the Roman road from Poole Harbour to Bath? You can hear a mysterious echo at one spot in the garden, and I always imagine there was an Agricocacola stall here, where the centurions pulled up and had the local tart.

The library bit, once my only sitting-room, was added on about 1900. Then I built on the present sitting-room beyond. To reach it you have to go down two steps. These are flanked by piers. I had read somewhere about someone rounding off the sharp corners of new-built piers, so I was pleased when Lincoln Kirstein said, 'They look as if they've been there for ever.' Black and white is the colour scheme. I found these lengths of material which was used to make sugar bags in Aleppo. They are of coarse white cotton, crudely printed in black with geometrical patterns, no two lengths quite the same; and they provided curtains for all three rooms.

The quite ordinary oak Victorian dining-room chairs are covered in black linen. I designed – and Alan, the village blacksmith, made – the elementary sideboard to hold a slab of slate. There is a heater underneath. The black *papier-mâché* trays were a present from my dearest cousin. The Sheffield plate candlesticks were a wedding present to my parents – they are hell to clean. I bought the round rosewood pedestal dining-room table in Bath in 1957. It was £8. If you are six there is no room for side-plates, so five is ideal. I so much prefer general conversation, anyway. Because of the pink quarry tiles in this room and the next I had always vaguely thought of the cottage as the sort of place a King of Naples might have stopped at, to eat an enormous picnic, while hunting. So when the framer Gibello, entirely off his own bat, framed the Jean Hugo landscapes in an unheard-of cork veneer, I thought he must be psychic, because this suggests those marble frames made for the sculpted 'pictures' hung in half-outdoor rooms, such as an orangery. Hugo's Stratford and Cotswold views were the first sketches in gouache for great screens twelve feet high, which, in my Shakespeare Exhibition, were to lead the young adventurer across country to Oxford, on his way to London.

Hugo married my greatest friend, Lauretta Hope-Nicholson; and when I bought this cottage he offered to design a rug for the sitting-room – now the library – which Lauretta would work. I asked if it might be black and white, with two shades of pink because of the quarry tiles, and perhaps ochre. He added a touch of Garter blue and made an unpredictable, untypical, almost Aztec design. The rug is eight feet square: it took Lauretta three years to work in double cross-stitch. I suppose it is the most wonderful present anyone ever had. To use up left-over wool, Jean designed cushions with stylized fountains and trees, and these were stuffed with the fleece of his own sheep. The dull old desk, at which I wrote many articles for the *Sunday Times*, was my great-grandfather Buckle's. (Nowadays I work at a much-too-small table in my bedroom.) Two of the odd narrow little bookcases were my great-grandmother Sandford's and used to be white and gold; I ordered two copies from Mr Johnson's admirable cabinet-maker in Shaftesbury; and Margot Burry marbled the lot. The straw Japanese cabinet I bought for £5 in that lane leading from Charing Cross Road to what has become Chinatown. It hides the back of the television. The *cloisonné* vases, which I turned into lamps, were bought for £20 from a lamp shop in Monmouth Street. To support them I designed the iron stands in what I thought was an 1880-ish asymmetrical way (as if they were made of bamboo) and they were perfectly realized by blacksmith Alan. Their tops, ordered specially for me in dark green marble, were a present from Marie Hugo and her husband David.

And so down to the sitting – or TV – room, which is to me what his empty theatre was to King Ludwig II, a Garden of Earthly Delights, and where I eat supper on a tray. It is hung only with drawings, so all the colour is in the loose covers and Turkish and Abyssinian rugs. The (Victorian) bolection stone chimneypiece was from John Teed at Bradford-on-Avon. One table came from Melksham, one from Stockbridge, one from Geoffrey Bennison of blessed memory, and the pair of octagonal coromandel-wood tables from Mr Johnson. The looking-glasses of straw, brass and black leather were made expressly to match the Japanese cabinet by Pauline Whitehouse. The drawings are mostly portraits of friends by friends, or nudes by friends. Some of the nudes were friends too. The John is of Lauretta; the Cocteau is of her husband Jean. The Hockney is of Beaton, who left it to me. Derek Hill did the portrait of George Harewood for me as a present. The Bachardy is of Astrid Zydower, the greatest living sculptor. There are what my mother calls *un*-likenesses of me by Rosoman, Hockney and Tsarouchis.

At sixty-eight, when one is just beginning to learn to write and may become senile tomorrow or tomorrow or tomorrow, everything is sacrificed to work – except, of course, pleasure. So I have no wives (who might introduce floral cretonnes), no dogs, no cars and no servants. I had one divine girl who cleaned, called Tess of the D'Urbervilles, but she suddenly bought the local delicatessen for £100,000. Other ladies tended either to have problems with children or to disappear without explanation, perhaps fearing sorcery or rape. I don't really mind a few cobwebs; and when someone is coming to stay or to dinner I dash round with a duster, muttering curses.

But I count my blessings, comparing myself with, say, neighbour Beckford. I can enjoy good productions of Shakespeare plays without moving from my sofa. I can breakfast at home and lunch in Florence, seeing the great gates of Fonthill and Stonehenge on my way to the airport, the Alps, Pisa and the Michelangelo tombs of my Medici relations – all in one day. I can hear any Mozart opera or piano concerto, performed far better than Beckford ever heard it, just by pressing a button. When the music stops and I go to bed between twelve and one there is total silence. Not a mouse stirring. Is there any greater luxury than that?

Above Part of the long room, with the tile-and-wood floor
copied from the nearby monastery.
Overleaf The balcony at the other end of the room, under
which many books are housed.

QUENTIN CREWE

FRANCE

At home, when I was young, decoration was not a topic of conversation. The most that was ever said on the subject was on the rare occasions when my father would announce, 'I think I'll tell them in the estate yard to paint the morning-room.' My mother would say, 'Oh yes, that will be nice.' There were never any discussions about colour or wallpaper or anything of that sort. Rooms were painted or papered in exactly the way they had always been done. My father would have regarded talk about décor as deeply suspect.

On the other hand, for various reasons, we had certainly twice, possibly three times, as much furniture as the house could accommodate. The ballroom and the big dining-room were piled high with whatever could not be fitted into the rooms we used. These stacks of furniture were a sort of challenge to my father, making him restless. Whenever there was a pause in his regular pursuits – no shooting, no fishing, no trees to be cut down – he would move furniture.

'Those Dutch pictures look a bit dull. Why don't we put some Italian ones there?' my father would say. So pictures were moved, which meant exchanging all the furniture, possibly even the use of the room. 'Let's have the dining-room in the library from now on.' For days we would labour. I don't think any aesthetic purpose governed these decisions. It was a way of using up energy.

The contradictions involved in always painting the rooms in the same way, but forever moving the contents around, unsettled me for life. I have had many rooms in many houses, but almost none of them, with the exception of two bathrooms, has seemed wholly satisfactory.

Part of the trouble is that I have dreadful taste. It is the choosing that is the problem here, not the final judgement. I choose some carpet, curtains and wallpaper and have them laid and hung. Then it is that my real taste comes into play. I am the first to see that what I have chosen is perfectly hideous. I remember with crippling shame a bedroom with purple velvet curtains and yellow walls.

This situation, naturally, induces a lack of confidence. I am inclined to seek other people's advice. I have too many of my father's genes ever to contemplate employing a decorator. Apart from anything else, I do not like a house or a room which looks as if it has been done up. I see no reason for things to match or agree too closely. I prefer a room which looks as if it just happened that way. A decorator's room is like a too-carefully dressed woman. Rooms, like women, should look as if they would not mind if one ruffled their hair a little. (The only decorator I did employ once, for a kitchen, put the marble slab over the radiator.)

None the less, being nervous, I ask for other people's opinions. It might be all right if it were just one person's advice but, like a hypochondriac, I confuse myself still further by asking everyone who comes to the house what I should do.

Recently, I have found myself in an entirely novel position. I have come to live in a house which has only one room of any significance. I have never been particularly concerned about bedrooms. Dining-rooms, although I have had nice ones, have always seemed wasteful. The rooms I have minded about have been bathrooms and sitting-rooms. Now, this house has a pleasant enough bathroom with spectacular views, but it is small. All rooms, in my opinion, should be big.

The only big room in the house is the sitting-room and, in many ways, it comes close to perfection in my eyes. The room was originally an entire house in a minute hamlet. It was a semi-detached cottage – two up and two down. It is built on steeply sloping land so that both the upper storey and the lower storey had doors at ground level.

The room dictated by its nature what could or could not happen. There were four windows. To add more or to enlarge them would ruin the stone exterior of the building. There was a rough concrete floor. As this room was to be knocked into the next house, some access was for various reasons essential at the upper level. A balcony or gallery was the only good solution. So then, a shell, about fifteen feet high on one side and eighteen on the other. In length, about thirty-two feet; in width, eighteen feet narrowing considerably to about fourteen feet. The sloping roof had exposed joists and, above them, flat tiles – a simple Provençal style not to be interfered with. The austerity of it appealed to me; I have never liked the florid, at least to live with. The restrictions were wonderful in that they stopped me rushing out to buy something regrettably ugly.

The wallspace was too great to allow any ideas of colour or patterning which might have tempted me into error. They were far better left as they were, covered with what the French call *crépie*, a half-rough stucco of nondescript colour. The floor was a chance to go wrong, but luckily I had the right advice. Carpets are wholly impractical in a place which is dust-ridden for nine months of the year and muddy the rest of it. Tiles, which are pleasant in the summer, are cold in winter.

The nearby abbeys of Senanque and Thoronet have floors of tile and wood in simple patterns. The combination somehow relieves the chill of tiles and is more practical than boards alone. It also looks pretty. We copied the monks.

The heating of this room is difficult, but there was in it a rough industrial oil-stove, somewhat like a Dalek in appearance. Its capacity to heat the room, and much of the rest of the house, economically was undoubted. After numerous consultations of contradictory opinions, I kept it. A dangerous period followed. Should we hide the Dalek? Or should we promote it, as it were, giving it pride of place?

The drawings were many and varied. One drew a pillared temple of Mithras to enshrine the stove; another had a tangled, steel spider's web for it to sit in; a third wanted to build something out of Chenonceaux to lose it in. In the end, we made a wide, stone, arch-like fireplace. Its top is level with the balcony at the other end of the room. The stove sits under the arch, neither hidden nor promoted. The arch is a little grandiose, perhaps, but it has the great advantage of making that end of the room seem much wider than it did before. That I like it so much makes me think it is probably a mistake as far as taste goes. I like the balcony too; probably because it is a trifle

baronial rather than because it is so elegantly functional, which, I am told, is why I should like it.

The first hurdles, thus, were easily surmounted. A balcony, a pretty floor and a slightly immodest arch.

Next, what to put in the room? First, books. They were easy as the balcony made a natural place underneath it for bookshelves. After that, I had a problem. I do have a number of possessions – paintings and furniture. Some time ago, I came to the conclusion that possessions were demanding; I should be rid of them. So I scattered them about among an appreciative family and felt free. Now I looked at this room and felt bereft.

I did not need much, I thought. What I needed were one or two big things and several big pictures. They also had to fit in to some degree with the Provençal simplicity of the place. I clawed back, from a mildly less contented family, some of my possessions.

Not much furniture. A large modern sofa and two armchairs, a plank of a desk (no drawers, otherwise letters go into them and never get answered) and a huge Italian wedding chest, decorated with dragons. The pictures, I decided, had to be seventeenth-century. Eighteenth-century would be too fussy. I brought a dozen, mostly portraits.

They look a little strange, but not too strange. A Lord Chief Justice, a Speaker of the House of Commons, James I, a Bishop, Nell Gwynne. How puzzled they would be, I think as I look at them from the balcony, to find themselves hanging in a farm cottage in Provence. A country house (Jacobean), a Neapolitan picture of Abraham and the Angels, a Dutch cathedral interior. The seventeenth century was remarkably adaptable in its appeal.

They give me a sort of reassurance, these familiar pictures. Then, on a chair under the arch, there is a plaster saint, from a demolished church at Banyuls, just in case anything looks too serious.

As a room, it is wonderful to work in, neither too open nor too shut away. For music it is perfect. For entertaining it is a little cramped at the narrow end, which is the natural end to sit. It suffers perhaps from the many ways in which it is used. In the summer my children regard it as a beach hut for the pool. For the rest of the year I think of it as a drawing-room.

Perhaps I should have, like my father, endless changes of furniture to cater for every mood of the year.

THE DUKE OF DEVONSHIRE

DERBYSHIRE

Above The Duke at work. On the desk is one of the lamps
taken from the main library at Chatsworth.
Opposite The view of the garden with the River Derwent
beyond and Capability Brown's undulating park.

When asked to write about the room of my choice I had no hesitation in selecting my sitting-room at Chatsworth.

Prior to the 6th Duke's time it was the breakfast-room. Its decoration was described by him as atrocious. He employed a Mr Crace to do it up, and when finished he described it as a mixture of a decoration for an old manuscript and a café in the Rue de Richelieu in Paris. The ceiling is decorated with flowers which surround murals of great poets. Since the 6th Duke made it into what he called the Lower Library it has been lined with books. In the last century they were rare and ancient volumes, now transferred to the main library on the first floor and facing east. I will return to the books at present housed there later.

The room has two windows facing west, thereby catching the afternoon and evening sun. They look out over the garden laid out in the last century with the river beyond and the undulating park landscaped by Capability Brown. Its fault as a room is that the chimneypiece is in the short north wall. Ideally a sitting-room has the fire in the long wall. But the chimneypiece itself is of fine marble superimposed upon a looking-glass some ten feet broad and running the full height of the room.

The furniture is a mixture. In front of the fire there is a large scarlet leather and mahogany sofa. In my grandfather's time this was in the smoking-room or Stag Parlour, as it used to be called. It is shabby and not particularly comfortable but I have grown used to it. I have brought a modest armchair from Bolton Abbey. Here I sit to read the papers, which I spend a great deal of time doing. In the centre of the room there is a satinwood table on which stand the drinks tray and various racing magazines, including the current edition of the *Racing Calendar*.

By the southernmost window is my writing-table. This is where I deal with my letters and dictate to my secretary. It is a nice table but nothing outstanding. The great Lord Burlington's table is in the house and I would dearly like to use it but it is too small. It is a sign of efficiency that the competent man requires a small desk which is always impeccably tidy. Mine is large and chaotic. In theory it has the usual in, pending and out trays, but these are rarely in their correct order and lie for the most part neglected and dust-ridden. There are two lovely library lamps taken from the main library and at night they shed a warm and comforting glow. I have collected a number of souvenirs which surround the blotting paper. These range from a medallion of the Crescent at Buxton, given to me during the two years I was Mayor of the town, to a gilt knotted bow, a present from Eunice Shriver, President Kennedy's sister, as a token of thanks for purchasing a painting on her behalf. There are a number of sentimental mementoes, in particular a lovely carved ivory rose and a lapis lazuli mineral egg. To hold paper clips and rubber bands there is another present which I value greatly, a shagreen box, and the hoof of a stag shot many years ago in Killarney. To my immediate right is a bronze bust of the 6th Duke whom I admire most among my forebears. Finally there are photographs and small trophies associated with my ventures on the turf.

It is now more than twenty-five years since we moved to Chatsworth, and I have acquired a vast quantity of what my elder daughter describes as 'glut'. Much of it should be thrown away, but my experience of throwing things away is that you tend to get carried away and throw away things that afterwards you regret. Therefore the drawers of my table get fuller and fuller. In theory each drawer has a special purpose, one for estate matters, another to do with letters concerning charities I am associated with, a third pertaining to my activities in horse-racing. There is one which I keep secret from my family where I store minor works of art, some with family connections. These I deliberate over as to which of my family shall receive them in my will.

To the right of where I sit is a fine mahogany table also with drawers, and here I keep the cellar book, wine merchants' catalogues and, most important, bulb growers' catalogues. On top of this table is the scarlet leather box which carried my private papers when I was Minister of State at the Commonwealth Relations Office in the 1960s. These boxes bearing one's name and post in gold lettering are the one 'perk' you are allowed to take away when you cease to hold office. Inside I keep important personal family papers such as my will and the deeds of various family trusts I have set up. In addition it is the repository for such letters in my possession that I consider might be of some historical interest. There are very few of these.

To the left of where I sit are the telephones and to the right the chair where Rosemary Marchant, my secretary, sits. When not in London I dictate letters to

The handsome marble chimneypiece superimposed upon a
large looking-glass that is the full height of the room.

her most mornings. I am a late starter and we usually begin when most people have gone to lunch. Owing to defects in my eyesight I do not find reading letters easy and so Rosemary reads them to me. She works in the next room, known as the Leather Room. It too is book-lined and contains a number of valuable bibles as well as Sotheby's and Christie's annual yearbooks complete since they were first issued. I use this room as a store for books and pictures I have bought but not yet hung or allocated to a shelf in my room or one of the visitors' rooms. Debo runs Chatsworth. My only jobs are the greenhouses, the cellar and the bedroom books. Beyond the Leather Room and further south is the front hall. This is a convenient juxtaposition, since people coming to see me have easy access and their arrival and departure bothers nobody else.

To return to my sitting-room. Not very long ago I was being interviewed by a journalist who repeatedly referred to it as my study while I called it my sitting-room. Finally he asked me why I called it that rather than my study, to which I replied, 'Because I sit in it more than I study in it.'

In spite of my eyes I still collect books avidly. My ambition is to create a contemporary library that would give someone of reasonable intelligence many happy hours of reading. I have concentrated largely on books written since 1900 or autobiographies and biographies of people who have died since 1900. The chief collectors' items are the complete first edition, including the novel and the pamphlet on India, by Sir Winston Churchill, and the complete run of *Horizon*. Fiction foreign and English is represented. I have gone further back than this century in this section. I have nice editions of Flaubert, Maupassant, Chekhov, Dostoevsky, Balzac, Proust, Tolstoy, Turgenev and Ibsen. America is represented with the beautiful pocket edition of Henry James – this would not be complete without the kindness of Frances Partridge who had the one missing volume and with immense generosity gave it to me – Edith Wharton and Scott Fitzgerald. Modern Russia is represented by Gorky and Solzhenitsyn. There is also the complete Novel Library published just after the war by Hamish Hamilton. It is now something of a collectors' item. Its list of titles is of the highest order. The mainstays

of English fiction are Trollope and Brontë, Saki, Kipling and Galsworthy, as well as Conrad, Shaw, Wells, Greene, Maugham, Waugh, Aldous Huxley, Arthur Koestler, Elizabeth Bowen, Anthony Powell, Iris Murdoch and Muriel Spark.

One of the problems of collecting a library is how to catalogue it: should it be by the author or should it be biography, letters and fiction? A shelf of which I am proud is that of the books on the First World War. Of course it is not complete but I have a considerable collection. In just the same way as the names on war memorials show far greater loss of life in the First World War compared with the Second, so does the number of books written on them. My Second World War shelf is not yet full. My particular joy is the disaster shelf. Again there must be many omitted. It covers such subjects as the San Francisco disaster, the Black Hole of Calcutta, the great Tay Bridge rail disaster, down to the great baccarat scandal, a fascinating book on the card scandal in which Edward VII when Prince of Wales was involved. There are shelves for India under the Raj and our African colonies. Literature on the latter I have found hard to come by. Books by friends have their space. Finally, since it is one of my great interests, the south wall contains a record of every flat race run since 1775. Below these is a full set of Ruff's *Guide to the Turf*.

Anyone reading these lines will immediately think of appalling gaps in my collection. I am aware of this and happy that it should be so in that I look forward to collecting books in the years that lie ahead. It would be fearful if this absorbing hobby had come to an end.

Modern means of communication are not neglected in the room. Around the fireplace are a television set, a selection of wireless sets, one for each of the four frequencies, and a gramophone.

Flowers have their place. There is always a sweet-smelling cut-leafed geranium on the satinwood writing table; others are seasonal, ranging from Paper White narcissi in the winter, to a variety of orchids, and amaryllis in the spring, but never chrysanthemums.

My sitting-room at Chatsworth reflects my life. Since major decisions concerning my family and the estate are taken there I, with *folie de grandeur*, nickname it 'The Oval Office'. I love my room.

In front of the fire is the old scarlet leather
and mahogany sofa removed from the Stag Parlour.

CHRISTOPHER GIBBS

OXFORDSHIRE

My great-great-grandfather died in Venice in 1844. He was from Devonshire, a banker brought up in Spain by his merchant-venturing father, and a railway pioneer and friend of Brunel's. Three months before he died, he had inherited from distant spinster cousins estates in Hertfordshire and Oxfordshire; and it was to Oxfordshire, to the ancient tumbledown church of St Michael and All Angels at Clifton Hampden, on a rocky bluff above a ferry over the Thames, with thatched cottages clustered beneath and along the river, that his embalmed body, escorted by his valet, was brought by sea while his widow and children travelled back overland, exploring cathedrals and art galleries as they moved slowly north.

The eldest boy was twenty-three, blue-eyed, dark and handsome, scholarly, devout, ambitious and an apostle of the new Anglo-Catholic fervour sweeping through the Church. He shot and hunted and fished and in the evenings illuminated vellum genealogies and missals, and his first act on inheriting was to restore the church and to build a new house next door for Uncle Joseph, who held the living, both with the aid of Gilbert Scott, the rising architect of the Tractarian gentry. He lived at Aldenham in Hertfordshire and in a Decimus Burton villa in Regent's Park, was Member for the City of London and Governor of the Bank of England, and throughout his life would return to Clifton Hampden for the partridge shooting, to plant woods, to enrich and beautify the church where his father and mother were buried, to build a pretty Gothic school and a lovely brick bridge spanning the river, giving work to the unemployed and closing the vista from the garden.

In 1864 he added a wing to the house in which I now live, and here it is that I read and write and watch television. A succession of priestly uncles and cousins succeeded one another until 1904 when my widowed great-uncle came to live here, again enlarging the house and redecorating it inside with Adam-style fireplaces, gay with De Morgan tiles, replacing the earlier ones of stone and marble; wallpapers by Morris and Bodley refreshed the vicarish walls, and books, furniture, paintings and trees were moved across from Hertfordshire. It became very much a man's house, of barometers and barographs, endless maps on rollers, clubs from the South Seas, fossils dug up on the estate under glass domes, sixteenth-century maiolica, medieval ivories and Persian carpets, and so it was when my parents arrived when I was a child to bring the sweetness and light and the eighteenth-century furniture that they preferred. Regency stripes covered Morris paper, linens from Peter Jones and cottons from Fortuny replaced the rich sombre curtains and covers, oaken doors were painted white or grey, fossils, maps and ethnographical toys were sent to jumble sales or put in the stables, and anything else deemed too precious for coexistence with six rowdy children went up to Christie's and paid for holidays and treats.

I inherited a house half empty and quite shabby, and began to sort and shift what was left and to pick away at the rooms, replacing the dainty Adam fireplaces, ripping out later fitments, bringing the rooms back to the scale and shape they started life with, forming my own room by piercing the walls to a small library, hanging the opening with eighteenth-century double doors *tromped* with books, raising the ceiling, revealing the pitch-pine rafters and stripping and pitching shutters and door cases. Bookshelves came from Wadham College, in disgrace with the planning officers for ripping out their library fittings, and in the lesser part of the new room, a fireplace was made of bits and pieces I had put by; eighteenth-century stone surround and wooden pediment, tiles from sixteenth-century Turkey and eighteenth-century Delft (these from an old house in the village). We put up the Morris Willow paper which is the one paper I really love and began to juggle with paintings and furniture.

It is not an easy room to furnish but it is a lovely one to live in. The stone mullions give on to the garden, which falls quickly to the invisible river, forty feet below and a long view over water meadows and fields to the Wittenham Clumps that John Nash loved to paint and the blue spine of the Chilterns. I keep a log fire burning when I am there, in the stone fireplace with its curious dog-toothed arch, and over it I have hung a painted Chippendale overmantel from Aldenham.

I live in London during the week, two chaste mid-green rooms in Albany, sky-blue ceilings with eighteenth-century wall to wall Turkey carpet below and white Henry Holland fireplaces topped with plain old mirrors facing one another. It is elegant, simple, emptyish and there are a few beautiful things to bring it to life, but home in the country is where the heart is and it seems much more difficult to bring it to perfection, to achieve the graceful harmony and beauty one must insist upon. There is a modesty about the rooms which makes them easy to choke and clutter; and making a room comfortable for oneself does not mean it is comfortable for others too. I love big bits of furniture and move them around relentlessly searching for the ideal. Lighting too is a problem. Most modern lamps are hideous, and Ming pots with card shades, which I like best, are hard to come by. Picture lights are a great help, and I shall soon make pools of light round favoured paintings – an old parson ancestor in his painted rectory study for a start.

So my room is really just for me with all the secret things that speak to me of life and love and anchor me down here, family relics, things I have always known set off by things that are perfect for their purpose. My favourite books are there for endless reordering and there are old watercolours of the church and river and fields outside mixed up with the family and their houses. Now I am steeling myself to bring in my toy cupboard, the glazed Georgian bookcase that contains treasures from childhood onwards, souvenirs and presents, talismans and relics, a paper cabinet of curiosities, of a whale's eardrum jostling a twelfth-century reliquary, bits of mummy propped up on a Cycladic pestle, my parents' medals jumbled up with coral, shells, coins and fossils.

A dream of a day when all is still, a place for everything and every thing in its place, no need or inclination to shake up the old kaleidoscope again. I think it is not too far away, and by the time that dotage is upon me I will have stopped worrying about resolving the disparate elements in the room that is the mirror of my life, although I hope there will always be a few perfect flowers from the garden and the fields and the wood beyond, to stuff into little glasses and bring nature's brilliance into the mix, and pretty postcards and photographs from thoughtful friends to garnish chimneys and tuck into mirrors and pictures, constant cherishings and tendings till the day I drop – I hope into a comfy armchair of faded Morris linen.

Previous page The walls are covered with William Morris willow-pattern
wallpaper.
Right Old paintings, drawings, engravings and so forth smother
the walls: all are very personal.

SIR JOHN GIELGUD

LONDON

For an actor, his dressing-room, in my case at any rate, is the centre of his existence during the hours he is committed to spend in it. So I can honestly call it my favourite room, though its features, in the many hundred different ones I have occupied over more than sixty years, must necessarily vary enormously from one theatre to another.

Of course, in my early days, I was always obliged to share a dressing-room with other actors, and was immensely gratified to have reached the privilege, in the early 1920s, of being given a room to myself, with my name proudly displayed upon the door.

My favourite room is in my favourite London theatre, the Haymarket. Although ideally it is preferable to dress as close to the stage as possible, this particular room is situated at the very top of the theatre, with a long flight of stairs leading up to it. It is almost like a small flat, with an ante-room and bathroom leading out of the main room, which has windows looking on to Suffolk Street far below.

There are plenty of shelves and cupboards, chairs, a sofa and a writing desk – even, until recent times, a coal fire in winter – and it is therefore possible to install oneself there comfortably, even occasionally in the daytime when there is no performance.

Here I dressed for a number of years in various productions, and in 1944, when the buzzbombs were such a disagreeable interruption, I would firewatch several nights a week, sleeping in my dressing-room at intervals. Garlands Hotel, only a few yards away, was hit and finally completely destroyed in two successive air raids, and I dreaded lest the theatre – so happily constructed, but mostly in wood and plaster – should also become a victim. I always wondered, too, if I should meet the famous Haymarket Ghost (said to be a famous old actor) during the watches of the night, but I never succeeded in seeing him, though Margaret Rutherford once claimed that she did.

The privacy of a star dressing-room gives its occupant a very pleasant promise of relaxation although the routine of making-up, now a much simpler pro-

Sir John Gielgud is seen nostalgically contemplating his old dressing-room at the Haymarket Theatre which he occupied for so many years, including those eventful war ones.

cess than was once thought necessary, demands the necessary tedium of looking at one's face in the glass for half-an-hour or so. But this is perhaps a less depressing prospect than the similar routine while shaving every morning.

The other London theatres in Shaftesbury Avenue and Charing Cross Road, mostly built at the turn of the century, are fortunately pretty well equipped with spacious and convenient dressing-rooms, whereas at Stratford-on-Avon, and more recently at the mammoth new houses at the National and the Barbican, they are amazingly ill-designed, cramped and uncomfortable. One cannot imagine that the plans for them could have been passed by experienced eyes.

The Broadway theatres in New York are, for the most part, equally gloomy and claustrophobic, while in Philadelphia I once played in a theatre where the dressing-rooms had been forgotten altogether, and the actors had to content themselves with rooms on the other side of the street and toil along a passage underground in order to reach the stage.

But I have always looked forward to arriving at the stage door, well before curtain time, to find my dresser laying out my dressing-table and costumes in correct order, to put on a dressing-gown, open my mail, and sit before the mirror knowing exactly how long I need to prepare for my performance. Even in times of great stress, nervousness, despondency, failure or success, my dressing-room is a refuge from outside interference and I even resent it when the telephone rings.

In the old days I always anticipated the callboy's knock with a mixture of pleasure and dismay, although that long-established character has now ceased to exist, and the insistent barking of the Tannoy system which has replaced it is for me a most unattractive and impersonal substitute in this progressive world.

With regard to dressing-room visitors I have rather mixed feelings, knowing that they can often mislead one into supposing that a performance has been very successful, when it has been nothing of the kind. They feel they must attempt to be tactfully complimentary at all costs, and one is apt to be suspicious if they are unduly enthusiastic. Interviewers with tape-recorders, long-forgotten acquaintances, insincere flatterers, importunate authors with their manuscripts, and the occasionally impertinent unknown fan — these are occupational hazards, and one needs a devotedly tactful dresser to deal with them and ration their intrusions for as short a time as possible. One is vain enough to be somewhat disappointed if no one comes to the dressing-room at the end of the performance. So long as people have the sense not to outstay their welcome.

The traditional ghosts at the Haymarket and Drury Lane are curious reminders of the great players who appeared in those theatres so long ago. At Her Majesty's and Wyndham's I dressed in rooms once occupied by Herbert Tree and Gerald du Maurier, and I felt proud to use those rooms so many years afterwards. And, in the last play in which I appeared in London, I found myself working for the first time in the Duke of York's Theatre, where I had seen my very first play, *Peter Pan*, when I was still a boy. So that the rooms backstage will always have a particular nostalgia for me, especially in the West End of London, where I so longed to appear and finally achieved that ambition over so many years. Will my own ghost linger in some of those dressing-rooms one day, I wonder?

As stage dressing-rooms go this is a luxurious one. It has a sofa-bed
and plenty of room for books, and until recently a coal fire in winter.

THE
EARL OF HAREWOOD
YORKSHIRE

I f the Englishman's home is his castle, the converse could be asked: Is his castle his home?

When I was a little boy, we used to stay at Harewood for Christmas with my grandparents, motoring the dozen miles from Goldsborough where we lived. At Harewood, we found hipbaths in front of a roaring fire, lots of older relations, and we plunged into all the traditional Christmas stuff, from log fires, games, walks through the woods and sometimes snow, to Christmas pudding and a touch of overeating. Everything seemed to be centred on one very big room in the middle of the house, where grown-ups congregated and towered over you, whose great potted palms dominated one of its ends, and at whose door Father Christmas knocked around six o'clock on Christmas Eve.

I suppose I was at first rather in awe of this large room, but then everything at Harewood was bigger than things at Goldsborough. At the same time I felt somehow at home in it. To a very small child the two things were not necessarily as contradictory as they sound. When a year or two later after my grandfather's death we came to live at Harewood, this room remained the centre of the house, though my parents banished the palms, antimacassars began to disappear off the backs of chairs, and the furniture was re-arranged. But the feel of the room was not much changed and as I grew older I began to love it, not just as the place where we played bagatelle while waiting for meals, where we sat after them, where chocolates were kept for children to eat – 'just one!' – while grown-ups drank their coffee, where in winter we played cards after tea, and from which we sallied forth on to the terrace in summer through the usually open French windows, which were as much the natural route into the gardens as the front door on the opposite side of the house was for more wintry expeditions either by car into Leeds or Harrogate or for a walk – not just for these reasons but because it was an essential part of home, which we thankfully came back to after any excursion into the outside

Lord Harewood with his labrador in the spectacular library at Harewood House. The room was originally designed by Robert Adam in the eighteenth century and then altered by Sir Charles Barry, architect of the Houses of Parliament, in the nineteenth century. The great chimneypieces are by Adam.

The opposite end of the Library, showing the second Robert Adam
chimneypiece. The fine ceiling is a survival of Adam's work.

world and, with even more positive relief, at the start
of the holidays from school.

The room is now called the library and has been
since I can remember, but Adam designed it with its
coved and intricately decorated ceiling as something
less homely and intimate. Sir Charles Barry, the

architect of the Houses of Parliament, altered it for
my ancestor in the 1840s into the room it now is, with
Adam's originally more modest bookcases extended
and framed in hefty Victorian mahogany, and with
the room transformed into a family sitting-room.
The lounge they called it then, and so it is described in

early guide books of the nineteenth century, but in my time we thought of it as in every sense of the words a living-room, and, with the exception of the war years, used it that way to such an extent that it began gradually in my subconscious mind to assume the position its chosen refuge does to an animal, and became the room that for me most embodied home. There after the war's end we entertained visitors when they came to Harewood, and – much more important – there we continued to sit as a family to talk racing and cricket and music, read newspapers or listen to the radio when we weren't busying ourselves with something more active.

Curiously enough, all of us seemed to dislike the purplish paint on the walls into which were let the frames of two admirable early oils by Turner, and we used to plot an alternative to what we then thought of as the height of Victorianism. No move towards change had been made by the time the war came, and at that point the room was turned into a furniture store so that the rest of the house could become a convalescent hospital. In early 1947 the hospital finally left, but we had not re-deployed the furniture until after my father died the same summer, and our plans to redecorate the room came to fruition only later, partly because good quality paint was very difficult to get in those post-war years, partly because we couldn't make up our minds what to do.

In 1958 and after much discussion, we had concluded that a kind of dark terracotta was the right colour for the walls themselves, with variations on the same colour as background for the ceiling – the terracotta seemed to provide appropriate camouflage for the massive bookcases, not contradicting the rather splendid Victorian carpet and suggesting colours for the re-painting of the ceiling, which had faded away over the years to a shadow of what was presumably originally intended (no coloured Adam designs survive).

If a room is supposed to reflect the personality of whoever lives in it, then the library at Harewood reflects not just mine but the evolving personality of a family, though it is true that I prefer high rooms like the library and don't care overmuch for the egg-boxes you find in most modern buildings. I couldn't re-create this room in any other house I might live in, as its concept, decoration and scale are too grand. In one sense it has never been *my* room, because I have never filled it with my own books and particular

preoccupations, like gramophone records and music scores, and in another sense it is no longer my family's room, as this part of the house is open to the public and therefore closed to us for at least the period between Easter and the onset of winter, and in practice for longer. But in the months the house is shut to the public, my family again takes possession of it, enjoys its size, which is never overpowering, and its warmth, sits around the fire, reads and gossips just as we did before and after the war when my mother was alive and presumably generations did before that.

The library is big enough for a Christmas party to break up into different elements, and I wonder if my own grandchildren, as they play games or make confetti of the wrappings of their Christmas presents, are developing an affection for the library as I did at their age. For me, December and January are doubly welcome; not only do my sons and their families gather for Christmas or New Year, but moving back into the library confirms my affection for it and justifies my hunch when, after my mother's death in 1965, we decided to leave the main floor of the house as general living quarters and open it all to the public. That, I was then convinced, would keep the whole area alive and allow it to contribute, and I had only marginal regrets at moving to another part of Harewood. This was partly because living on a higher floor produced compensatory and very positive pleasure in the form of an uninterruptedly splendid view. What you can see from it is for me a major part of the pleasure a room can provide. As I write, I am looking out of the window of a much smaller room immediately above the library – rare at 6.30 in the morning in my case as I am a night, not an early morning, person – and I can see the black St Kilda sheep (a Harewood constant) dotted about the brilliant green between terrace and lake, and above all watch the bird activity of an early summer morning, ducks on the water, Canada geese honking away, and Capability Brown's landscape taking up middle and far distance with only a hint of Leeds no more than four miles to the south.

That's in spring and summer – and it's the view from another room. Returning to the library in winter involves a very special form of 'going home', more particular and even stronger than the general one of being in this part of Yorkshire, which I always feel. It is a room in which I have always found it very easy to live.

JOHN HARRIS

GLOUCESTERSHIRE

Our rooms are sleeping inside us. For most there is no awakening, or else it is left to some decorator to sound reveille, to be the womb substitute assembling the bits and pieces of life's detritus. We who awaken ourselves to an awareness of the room must disinter from long ago the first stirrings of a consciousness to the enveloping wall. For me it was a bedroom overlooking old brickfields and orchards, and I can recollect a window with a white wooden shelf upon which I had made my first arrangement: in the centre a large oval wax relief by Lucas based upon an ancient Greek coin, flanked by two bronze female figures. The Lucas was rare and fine, the bronzes no doubt Edwardian and bad. I cannot remember much more except that when I returned from military service in Malaya in 1951 the heat of the sun had folded the wax into half, irrevocably lost. No doubt the bronzes grace another's room.

I am next conscious of Paris in 1952 and slumming in the *vieux hôtels du Marais,* or old houses in other *arrondissements.* I was a bold young man quite unabashed at knocking on doors and penetrating to the private intimacies of what the French call *disposition.* Here occurred one of those confrontations that seen in retrospect are decisive in the formation of *le vrai goût.* I had written unannounced to Francis Watson, then Deputy Director of the Wallace Collection, who kindly replied, 'Go to see Richard Penard and his collection in my name.' Of course I did, and I often wonder if anything exists in Paris today as exquisite as that collection now dispersed in the Louvre or American museums. Richard had made it into a perfect demonstration of the beauty and desirability of *le style transitional.* It was faultlessly assembled, and by no means sterile as are so many of those collections of French furniture made by rich Americans who have more money than taste. Unlike them, Richard's soul had entered into the collection. Unconsciously he was conveying to me his secret of that spiritual rapport between the collector and the collected. He communed with the things he loved. He taught that the juxtaposition of one object to another is not only a matter of space, but of colour, shadow and texture, and that essential quality of being neighbourly. He recognized that whereas a terracotta would not sit harmoniously with a bronze, a piece of cream Capo di Monte would, as would a maiolica plate. Richard showed the value of light, indirect as well as direct, of low wattage bulbs, even of candles, and he expressed a loathing for the modern spotlight. I leave him with the memory of a nocturnal man whose guests were invited to come to his house at eleven in the evening, and at three or four in the morning, the best champagne and sticky cakes in Paris would be served. He would then close up and retire to a mattress set in an alcove on the landing of the stairs.

My pilgrimage had begun, the route taken to be marked by shrines, for the discovery of the extension of self into the objects collected is not unlike a religious exercise leading to revelation. I must now reflect as to where I paused and at whose shrines I worshipped. After Paris my pilgrimage took me to 20 Thurloe Square and Geoffrey Houghton Brown. How can one encapsulate the character of Geoffrey in a few lines? He is painter, decorator, antique dealer, peripatetic buyer of country houses, and devoted Catholic. He wandered from shop to shop effortlessly buying treasures. He conveyed the value of premonition in the chase, the necessity to act upon the gut feeling rather than hesitate with art-historical caution. His eye was a painter's working upon a room as upon a canvas, and surely there was no one who could seemingly, without care, throw objects together with such flair as he. His style is his own, always rich and often with pieces of the severe Boulle that he so loves. Throughout the thirties, and after the war, I suspect his professional decorator friends learnt much from him simply by a form of osmosis by contact. He would never confess this, for he is (alive as I write) a diffident man, but I can quote John Fowler, and Felix

Harbord always acknowledged Geoffrey's gift for arrangement. Today a generation of art dealers who have become bankers would be shocked by some of his effects, like the full-length Hudson-style portraits brought from the Claydon House sale in the fifties and cut down to make *trompe-l'œil* doors at nearby Winslow Hall, that Wren house saved by Geoffrey from the demolition men. What mattered was the effect. Only he could paint the revered eighteenth-century red floor tiles at Viviers green and yellow and get away with it! It was not a question of the value or rarity of an object, although in his rooms might be found a bidet belonging to the Duc de Penthièvre sitting under a James Moore table from Wardour Castle. It was different at my next shrine at Hungershall Lodge, Tunbridge Wells, long since gone and the altar desecrated by other owners. I mean Rupert Gunnis and his extraordinary collection.

Here was an experience more positively of the scholarly, art-historical kind, in a house with a dozen treasure cabinets and libraries. It was a collector's *horror vacui*, and Gunnis must belong to the same family tree as Horace Walpole at Strawberry Hill, or preferably Dickie Bateman at Old Windsor. For a Bateman, Walpole or Gunnis connoisseurship, the collector's sure instinct, and a love for the quixotic and odd, made a work of art out of the treasure cabinet. A Fugger in the sixteenth century arranged his objects in his *Schatzkammern* into a composition with the same rules that must make a painting succeed. Hungershall Lodge was an evocative amalgam of pictures, drawings, engravings, marbles, terracottas, bronzes, ceramics, waxes, enamels, silhouettes and needlework. Every inch of wall was loaded, every table covered. My memories are not only museological or of that rich and rare library, but of comfortable chairs, an abundance of scented flowers and orchids, and wicked conversation. He had an innate sense of style and I suspect he was an *éminence grise* behind the organization of country houses in the early history of opening to the public. There was

Parham and Blair Castle, Stratfieldsaye and Penshurst, Buxted Park and perhaps Eridge. The point about Hungershall Lodge was that without Rupert it would have been irrelevant. I can remember Christopher Hussey remarking soon after Rupert's death that the atmosphere of the house could not be conveyed to a *Country Life* reader without the attentions of its owner. How true this is, how right that the Penard and Gunnis collections were dispersed. Surely the soul leaves the collection as does life from the body of the collector. What a sadness is Count Seilern's collection now, how appropriate that Paul Wallraff's was sold, and let us hope that no curator will put Sir Brinsley Ford's collection into public aspic.

The wayside shrines that we pause at are few. We cannot worship without intimacy with the collector. Brinsley Ford's must surely be someone's shrine, but it was not mine for I have not paused there long enough. I stopped at Francis Watson's in Glebe Place to take in those layers of pictures and drawings, that bookcase shelf of *objets de vertù*, to imbibe the conversation of that discerning collector, and to wonder at the dozens of Jane's cats. I stopped too in Ladbroke Road to wonder at Charles Handley-Read's confection of Victorian art which he pioneered as a subject for collecting. He communed with every object, and his rooms glowed with the concentration of his devotion. It drove him to suicide. And finally I must not forget Stratfieldsaye, where architect the Duke of Wellington's own collector's instinct and Rupert Gunnis's flair for arrangement enriched the inheritance of the Iron Duke.

So the pilgrimage ends with one's Santiago de Compostela, my own room in Gloucestershire. It speaks for itself, and I can no more explain the grammar of my construction than can my friend Christopher Gibbs explain his ability to induce the patina of timelessness into his rooms. No doubt Christopher has his own shrines, but those who make the pilgrimage are few, the rest are pretenders: better they employ the decorators.

Previous page Part of John Harris's 'Santiago de Compostela',
where the subdued lighting creates a very special atmosphere.
Left Every inch of every wall is loaded and every table
covered with precious objects.

SIR NICHOLAS HENDERSON

WEST COUNTRY

('If Alvilde arrived I wonder if it would go like this.)

'Do I intrude?'

'Well, yes but . . .'

'You see I am much more interested in seeing rooms where people work or day-dream, than drawing-rooms. If only men wouldn't call them dens.'

'I don't.'

'Good, but this is where you read or write or whatever you do on your own?'

'Yes; it is also where I do nothing, and do it intently and alone.'

'I am sorry to break the spell; but you do see, don't you, how tempting it is to see what a man has on his desk, or his chimneypiece, on the walls and in his bookshelves; and whether he has a photograph prominently placed of his wife or his dog. They're bound to tell you something. After all they are not there for display.'

'Well, anyway, sit down do, here on the club fender if you want, back to the fire, warming your imagination, as the Gillray print above puts it with eighteenth-century subtlety, or do you prefer to prowl?'

'Is the club fender an essential part of your furniture?'

'Yes.'

'Then I'll sit on it.'

'You'll see why, warmth behind and a full view in front.'

'And that large Parliament clock above the sofa – essential too?'

'Yes; it tells the time but also reminds you that the passage of time is not the same as progress, because a spring in the clock is better than interruptable electric current and the tick is more reassuring than the digital twitch.'

'The barometer over there. Is that for use or ornament?'

'I can see you don't listen to the weather forecasts or you would know you have to rely on your own systems. The daily tap of my barometer tells me more than those patches of rain or sun stuck improvidently on TV charts.'

'That pyramid of bronze on the windowshelf – what purpose does it serve?'

'Oh, that's a fountain head. One day I hope to have a fountain to go with it. Got it in the Rastro in Madrid, the local Portobello Road.'

'Your room seems to be full of things picked up abroad, prints, books, objects . . .'

'Yes. I always saw it as a home for something which caught my fancy abroad, not that you will see any native art such as shrunken heads, tomahawks or elephant feet umbrella-stands. In fact most of my things are English – that looking-glass with a Turkish head, for instance, or the Staffordshire figures.'

'You seem to go in for things of a certain size.'

'I like furniture and objects to be large and un-brittle – of leather, wood, brass or marble – not decorative.'

'Why is it called the School House?'

'Because this room was the village school, at one stage of its history. Up there you'll see a photo of the pupils taken outside. They give me inspiration.'

'I'm struck by the way your room is crowded round the edges but seems empty in the middle, like a lawn surrounded by flower-beds.'

'I like to be able to walk up and down without knocking things over. As you will see, the carpet is anything but ancient Persian. I am always coming in from the garden with dirty shoes, I don't want to have to take them off all the time.'

'I suppose you do most of your work at that desk, but you seem to have another one on the floor landing just above.'

'If I have to write something I usually begin in an armchair and then find that it won't do so move to the desk. The one upstairs is meant for serious things.

This one, the partner's desk, is for muck, for paying bills and dealing with correspondence. But it doesn't really work out that way. In fact I do everything here at the big one and nothing at the other desk.'

'Which you reach by that cast-iron circular staircase?'

'Yes, my grandson loves it and keeps climbing it. It leads to the bathroom. Very necessary to have a bathroom near a study.'

'You mention your grandson being in here. That means that your room isn't sacrosanct. Do you welcome people in? Not me, I mean.'

'Yes; sometimes for a drink or to read the papers or to climb the circular staircase.'

'The furniture, pictures, the whole thing. Was it you? Or did you get advice – from Mary, for instance?'

'Oh yes, the Morris wallpaper – called Christ Church – and the way it covers ceiling and walls enclosing the room in a coloured envelope. I wouldn't have dared do that. It was Mary's idea. I don't claim infallibility in taste, only arrogance.'

'In what ways is your taste arrogant?'

'Well largely in what I don't have. But also I suppose in the non-pretty things that I need. The telephone which I like to have. The reading lights aggressively Christopher Wray so as to be sure that I can read properly. And the enormous waste-paper basket so that I can shy things into it from afar and it doesn't throw up at the sight of discarded Sunday papers.'

'Does the view matter? Do you find yourself gazing out of the window at your garden?'

'Frequently. But I like having the French windows open all day in the summer so there is no divide between indoors and out.'

'Yes, that's the impression your room gives. I notice your pots of bulbs everywhere. But also the amount of light you have. The ceiling is immensely high and there is a sense of airiness.'

'I hope that doesn't mean you're cold.'

'No, I realize you have a belt and braces variety of heating systems – log fire, electric stove and radiators. But I mustn't become too comfortable, or I'll stay. Let me, though, glance at where you look out to through the French windows. You give on to another little building in which there are three œil-de-bœuf windows that look much like portholes, then there is the barometer indoors and I notice a whole pile of maps. Doesn't it strike you all as slightly nautical?'

'Well, after all, an Englishman's room is his fo'c's'le.'

Previous page Large windows give plenty of light. The walls and ceiling are covered with a William Morris paper called 'Christ Church'.
Left The large decorative and unusual English looking-glass with a Turk's head engraved on it.

THE HON. DAVID HERBERT

MOROCCO

The small apricot-coloured card-room where David
Herbert spends much of his time.

In 1985 I find it difficult to know how to describe 'an Englishman's room'. In the old days it was easy: leather chairs, brass ashtrays attached to bands slung over the arms, pipe racks and cleaners, hunting prints, large dog baskets, preferably for labradors or retrievers, a grandfather clock, a few riding whips, a huge kneehole desk and probably a filing cabinet or two, a fender surrounding the fireplace on which you could sit, and the inevitable drinks tray with a decanter of whisky and port. In fact, 'Dad's den'.

Very few Dads have a den these days – most people are lucky to have one large communal sitting-room with either a 'dining area' or a kitchen-*cum*-dining-room. I am spoiled living in Tangier, where I have a devoted 'staff' (servant has become a dirty word) to look after me. I have a drawing-room, a smaller sitting-room leading off it, a garden hall, a card-room and a dining-room. The first two rooms are definitely unisex. The card-room, where I spend most of my time, is I suppose a 1985 'Englishman's room'. Colour is important to me. The walls are dark apricot, the ceiling white from the middle of which hangs a silver William and Mary chandelier. A large bookcase covers one entire wall; over the chimney-piece hangs a Regency gilt mirror. The other walls are plastered with watercolours and drawings, some good, some middling, but none bad; there are so many, in all twenty-four, that it almost resembles a wallpaper: each one holds a memory for me.

In the middle of the room stands a round table covered with a velvet cloth of an indefinite colour, on which sits the canasta tray, the dice, the patience cards, an ashtray, my engagement book, a few pens and pencils, the novel I am reading, a vase of flowers and a notebook with 'DON'T FORGET' printed on it.

There is a French window that opens on to a small terrace where my 'mini' swimming pool is situated: it is invisible from the garden and only used by me. It is more of a 'basin' than a pool, as it was a cistern to catch the rain water before we were attached to the main water supply.

In one corner stands my television set, very important, as we get excellent programmes from Gibraltar relayed from London and also two very good Spanish stations.

In the corner opposite is a Regency writing-table, practically never used by me as I invariably write at the round table, but useful for guests who buy endless postcards and send them to loved ones at home.

I am forgetting the cat box filled with sand which sits under the writing-table. They seldom use it, being such clean animals, but sometimes in the night they do get a tummy upset like the rest of us and rush at once to their only loo.

I have had dogs all my life, but when about six years ago my two remaining ones died, I felt I couldn't face another at my age. A lady friend of mine living here, a cat lover, said, 'Why don't you try cats?' 'Cats!' I said, 'but I don't know cats and I think I heartily dislike them.' 'Do try,' she said. 'I don't wish to be rude, but they are so much easier to look after when you are getting on in years. No Outy Outy, no Walky Walky, and you will see that they will learn to love you just as much as a dog.' I tried and now could not live without them, they are so well fed and loved that they don't even glance at my birds.

My two minah birds take up the last corner of the room. They talk a great deal, sometimes gibberish, sometimes perfect sense, distracting me from anything I am doing: particularly helpful to me who am incapable of concentrating at the best of times. From the French window I get a view of my aviary which is full of coloured birds, cockateels Calypso, Rosella parakeets, Indian lovebirds, and a glorious brilliant red bird with blue wings which apparently comes from Peru.

When I am watching television in the evening in this room the five cats are dozing in the Hepplewhite armchairs (not leather), with comfortable lime-coloured squab seats, while the minahs chuckle away under their turquoise nightcover. Having said all this about my cats and birds, will the average reader still think it's 'an Englishman's room'? I don't see why they shouldn't, as Sargent, T. S. Eliot and so many great men through history have loved cats.

The room I am writing about is the smallest of the reception rooms. I don't like being by myself in a large room. I feel lost and am never sure that someone else isn't hiding behind a screen, sleeping in a deep armchair under a copy of *The Times* or peeping through a door when my back is turned. Perhaps this stems from being brought up at Wilton where the rooms are vast, and being pushed by Nanny into one of them, after tea, dressed in a silly little sailor suit, squirming with embarrassment as my mother told me to go and say 'Good evening' politely to those charming guests of hers – after which my brothers and I would sit around being asked ridiculous questions by bejewelled ladies, exclaiming in loud voices how sweet we were, or asked by some choleric old gentleman whether I wanted to be a soldier when I grew up. 'Oh darling Nanny, do rescue us,' we murmured under our breath. She always arrived on time and we ran out of the eighty-foot-long library whooping with joy and received a good ticking off next day from my mother for not saying good night politely. Perhaps this is my reason for liking small rooms.

I don't use the unisex rooms unless I have guests. The Englishman's room is seldom visited except by the chosen few: in winter I lunch at the round table, which can seat three others beside myself. I consider 'the dining-room' a dull room and useful only for large dinner parties or lunch parties, if the weather is bad. In the old days, with many courses and endless dirty stories told over the port and brandy, several hours were spent there; but in these days the average meal lasts such a short time, that a dining-room is just a waste of space.

The 'study' was a word my parents never used. I never knew exactly why except that it was considered middle-class; perhaps Nancy Mitford, if still alive, could have clarified this point. None the less I imagine, to the average household, the 'study' was the 'man's room', in fact his 'den', where he was never disturbed, except, perhaps, by a timid knock on the door by his wife to say that lunch or dinner were ready, or a terrified child summoned to be admonished for some grave misdemeanour. I have never employed a decorator and never will. Before I lived here, my home was the Park School at Wilton. That house in the woods was smaller than my present one but I am sure had the same atmosphere: I don't think one's taste changes unless, to appear young and 'with it', one decides to go modern. This is not a good idea for an older person. It is in fact a mistake, like putting a picture in the wrong frame. Another point is that you would have to change most of your possessions; this I could never do, as I feel a personal attachment to every piece of furniture, every picture and almost every object I possess.

Looking through the drawing-room to the card-room.

DAVID HICKS

OXFORDSHIRE

The bedroom window is framed by bookshelves.

The best kind of English rooms are those which contain a cosmopolitan collection of different pieces of furniture, books, drawings and objects, though somehow sympathetic to each other, in a space with a decorative theme, however simple, all of which goes to make up a cosy, interesting and individual atmosphere.

I grew up in a house with warmth and individually interesting things but with no feeling for style or originality; but at an early age I saw other people's houses which had far more ambience and character, more unusual contents than ours, which made me long to arrange rooms and to collect original furniture and accessories to make interesting interiors.

I was lucky eventually to possess the best of my parents' things and able also to make my own collection. I was very influenced, in forming my taste, by various friends and acquaintances, and by constantly making a choice between one alternative and another I found my own style.

When I was young I saw Renishaw and Belchamp, Guisnes Court and the Hamlet House, Althorp and Kelmarsh, the Malcontenta and Fiorentina and most of the great historic houses of England and many in France. Each house gave me an inspiration, however simplified my interpretation would be. It was all part of getting my eye in for proportion, scale, period, atmosphere, style arrangement, objects, furniture and pictures.

I think that English rooms are far less studied than American ones and far cosier than European rooms. It is hard to pinpoint exactly what it is that makes them more sympathetic, but it could be the clutter and the flowers and plants which most of us love to fill our rooms with, even in London. English rooms have not always been as eclectic as they are today. You only have to look at a Hogarth or a Devis to see how empty they were in the middle of the eighteenth century. I think it was when people started to travel for pleasure and to inherit from relations that the overcrowding of rooms started in the mid nineteenth century, and, apart from a thirties movement which in some houses cleared out a lot of accumulated possessions, this full look has been emulated widely – culminating in the somewhat false English country house look in the United States at the present time.

My room is a small white mezzanine library where I sleep, work and bath – it is exactly what I like most for the country – and I am surrounded by some of my favourite books and memorabilia.

I made it symmetrical with the window and wash-basin, surrounded by bookshelves, centrally placed opposite the bed. The bath is set at right angles in an alcove hung with coloured *Directoire* prints of medieval artefacts, flanked by two gothick hall chairs of 1820. The walls are painted vanilla, the Hicks carpet is a vermilion, beige and white basket weave design, and the Roman shade, half-tester bed and reading chair are of a black, ivory and sand-coloured nineteenth-century rose chintz. On the wall opposite the bath there are a pair of low marble topped bookcases on either side of my grandfather's Greek tomb topped mahogany clothes press. The bookcases have objects on them related by colour or form but disparate in 'provenance'. All the books are bound in vellum, beige or canvas. Some are large decorative sets but others are working reference books. The washbasin is set in the top of a third bookcase and the wide top holds more objects. It's reassuring to have books near the bed if one can't sleep, and in the early morning I love to look at one I haven't seen or read for thirty years.

On either side of the bed there is a pair of glazed gothick cupboards stuffed with valueless memorabilia. Three clockwork pigs which dance and play a drum, a flute and a violin, my great-grandfather's 'laissez-passer' for St Omer in 1818, a coffee cup rescued from the Salters' Hall after the blitz in 1941, views of Britwell painted on eggs by Mark Hampton, a cigarette box I painted in the Vanessa Bell manner when I was thirteen, cut-out silhouette photographs, a collection of penknives, etc.

Sitting up in bed I can see part of two sections of our garden epitomizing my attitude towards it – one the formal 'allée' of clipped hornbeam trees with hedges below and the other with ancient oaks beyond the wild spring garden with a classical urn separating them. I see partridges and pheasants and lots of sky.

I have in some ways re-created the kind of atmosphere of the dressing-room in our former house in the country but, the memorabilia apart, the ingredients are not the same; yet there is a similar ambience. The architectural drawings on the walls are different, the candlestick lights have opaque shades which give identical light as before, and the spotlight in the half-tester provides a reading light. I control the daylight with the Roman shade at the window.

My possessions mean a lot to me and after a disaster, being acquisitive, I would always start collecting again because I like organized clutter around me. On a desert island I would create table-scapes of *'objets trouvés'*.

It is my room, though because some of our books are in it the family naturally make forays into it during the day, but there is only one comfortable chair which discourages more than one intruder at a time. At night it is quite mine. When I travel I miss my bedroom, bathroom, bookroom and its splendid proximity to my beloved garden, its simplicity, the really comfortable bed with proper square goose down pillows, and Frank Brangwyn's 'Pageant of Venice', Paul Reilly's *Regency Architecture*, Roloff Beny's *India* and Rudolf Wittkower's *Bernini* very near at hand.

I very often wake at around 6.30 a.m. and my room has a marvellous atmosphere in which to work. I have a pen and pad permanently at my bedside so that as I go to sleep or as I wake I can note down last thoughts or the ideas that tumble forth as one wakes in the morning. The room faces south, so that I get sideways rays of sun from the left in the early morning and during the summer the blind must be down to keep the heat out during the day. It is, of course, a very personal room, and I imagine it would suit few other people, but for me it is perfect. I want nothing grander, larger or with better things in it – it suits my desire for simplicity and interesting contents and it is highly practical. It is also the complete opposite of the pretty, feminine rooms in one's friends' houses and of the stark desperation of most international hotels where I perforce stay on account of our international clients.

It was not hard to decide on which of our rooms I should write about because I think mine is very English and very personal. I think that the reason I like it so much is because it is very undecorated. I devised it to be constant. I simply put many of my favourite things together and it will stay that way for the rest of my life.

The bath is set in an alcove hung with coloured Directoire prints.

MILES HILDYARD

NOTTINGHAMSHIRE

I have chosen my own room, which is both sitting-room and office. When I came here aged thirteen it was given to me and my next brother as the Boys' Room. I think it had been my great-aunt's bedroom but she had died over twenty years before. It is on the first floor in the middle of the south front, sunny and warm with large windows looking over the park and lake. It is part of the solar of the medieval house, and a door leads on to the gallery of the library, which was the great hall. The gallery is lined with old books and stuffed birds. After the war I came home and it was my room until my father died in 1956. Then I gave it to my mother as it is the nicest room, and moved myself into the small library, which was my father's room. I didn't like this; it was dark and I had to be tidy. So I moved upstairs again into a large bedroom, which had been my parents', with windows on two sides and handsome arches on a third, not much room for cupboards but the most attractive room I have had here. A bell was put in from the back door. From there I migrated to the drawing-room below, turfed out the French furniture and installed a vast bookcase. The idea was that I could drink cocktails on the terrace, coal didn't have to be lugged up and ashes down, the dogs and farm men wouldn't dirty the staircase, I would know when people arrived at the front door, etc. In fact I don't think I ever drank on the terrace, the French windows wouldn't open and it is windy, and we took to using the back door.

When my mother died in 1978 I moved back again. In the meantime the room had become more civil-ized; yellow moiré wallpaper, nice chintz curtains. The pictures are mostly large watercolours and pas-tels of my grandfather and his brothers as children around 1850, the last children here before myself and my brothers, and of my mother. I hope they show in the photographs. There are two glass-fronted book-cases and I put in shelves. I put in the very large desk which moved round with me and in no time a terrific amount of paper clutter. I have friends who never have this lying about. I like to think they have offices

and secretaries hidden away, but I am afraid it is just my inefficiency. I hate throwing things away, and I have had to resign from various societies because their magazines, which I think most interesting, pile up so. I bury things on my desk for years. Last Christmas I found and accepted an invitation card to a party and the hostess telephoned to say she wasn't giving a party, in fact she was going away. I then remembered I had been to the party a year or two before. Since I gave up filing I make piles until there is enough for a suitcase and put it in my mother's clothes cupboard outside. This is not perfection, as at intervals I badly need something and have to write to my solicitor or whoever for a copy. I have filing cabinets, but they are full of farm papers which I can't bear to go through, and anyway they may be of interest in 500 years' time. My own interests go further back. I have written seven volumes of Flintham and family history; most of the work was on the eleventh to thirteenth centuries. I got bogged down in that period for many years. I employed a searcher in the Public Records Office who translated charters in a handwriting far more illegible than the originals (but not in Latin), and I made lists of endless peasants' and field names. This interest was nothing new. I messed at school with a Catholic and we drew coats of arms and looked up extinct baronies in the gallery of the School Library when we should have been trying to get into Pop.

I see there are some questions we are encouraged to bear in mind. Does my room reflect my personality? Yes. Absolutely. Do your possessions mean much to you? Yes. Do you regard your room as sacrosanct? I may say there are, I think, seven sitting-rooms in this house (small the HHA would say); the remaining six are tidy, polished and suitable for guests. However, my room has the only colour telly and insensitive children are apt to occupy it. Apart from one corner of the sofa the rest is occupied when I am there by dogs. It is the only room where they are allowed on the chairs (their decision, not mine).

Do I call a decorator in? Certainly not. My idea of a house is that new wallpaper, new curtains, etc., if ever, are once for a lifetime. I must admit, however, that everything in this house is perpetually on the move except in my room, so it must be sacrosanct.

Previous page This room, where the owner deals with his desk clutter, is kept generally very light by yellow moiré silk wallpaper.
Left A charming nineteenth-century watercolour of a family group.

DEREK HILL

My father bought the house in the early fifties and, although I have lived in Donegal for most of the time since then, one room could be referred to as Derek's room because of its containing so much of the clutter that I have accumulated.

The house was originally two little eighteenth-century workmen's cottages. In the 1920s they had been made into one house. Luckily I have been able to store my pictures there and to paint the occasional portrait in it. My family don't seem to complain.

Greta Garbo was once brought to tea with me in Donegal, and looking at the study's disarray, murmured in that unforgettable and deep voice of hers, 'Oh Derek, for the first time in my life I feel quite tidy.'

Rather the same condition applies to my allotted room in London.

The fact of never being inclined to throw things away does not help, of course, and a pyramid of might-be-useful used envelopes on the desk takes up a great deal of the writing space.

Above the desk table the light is shaded by a stained glass panel by Evie Hone, who did the great East window of Eton College chapel, and below this a Wemyss Ware tabby cat stares out in front of a Peter Lanyon gouache – rather reciprocating in its design the cat's head.

There are photographs of my parents' wedding, with a flock of bridesmaid aunts wearing huge white hats of bird of paradise feathers – one of the aunts having been the owner of the Wemyss Ware cat; there is also a photograph of my housekeeper, Gracie, in Donegal. A mask by Cortright hangs from a shelf over a pile of books and is flanked by more photographs of my hut on Tory Island where I paint during the summer months.

In a corner a Blue Wemyss Ware pig protects a figureless landscape by Lowry hung above it and silver glass funfair ornaments – once widely described to me as Thermos glass vases keeping the seated sow company.

Rugs have been brought home from Laghouat in Algeria, from Tabriz in Persia and from Constantinople, and chairs have Morris linens and cushions and stuffs from India and Italy hanging over them. Morris was responsible for the curtains, and some De Morgan tiles contribute to these Islamic-inspired patterns.

Then of course there are stacks of my own pictures of all periods – ones that I have refused to part with and that I herd around me like children in a family. A sketch head of Princess Liechtenstein done in Vaduz preparatory to the state portraits of her and her husband lean against a bookshelf, and a big harbour scene of West Town on Tory Island, showing the early Tau Cross, is below the skylight. Other small landscapes, done in Italy when I lived in Berenson's Villino for some years, sit on shelves with pieces of Irish Delft Ware between them, and a Russian teapot given me by Violet Trefusis above a little 'biscuit' figure of Shakespeare left to me in memory of Elizabeth von Hofmannsthal.

Everywhere there are souvenirs and mementoes and even some novelties (shops that sold objects described as such always fascinated me as a child): a piece of chewing-gum from Italy called Big Ball Bum – presumably named by a GI during post-war occupation – sits on an art nouveau saucer, which almost hides one of Bamforth's splendid postcard series – this one called 'The Wicked Girl of the Family'. Some drawings by Robert Byron, given to me by his sister Lucy, share a folio with my own drawing of Alfred Brendel and remind me of my annual visits to Mount Athos with James Lees-Milne.

Everywhere are these reminders of a lifetime. The French have a proverb, 'Il faut meubler l'intérieur de soi-même', and probably the accumulation somehow reflects character, like handwriting and its graphological explanations.

Hating to get rid of things probably represents some Freudian twist in me, and my wish to own something belonging to friends who have died is romantic and sentimental. Syrie Maugham's daughter gave me a rock crystal parrot that always stood on her mother's desk and reminds me that Syrie gave a luncheon party for my first exhibition when I was eighteen – a day when half the sophisticated world of Paris could be invited because of their being in London to view Princess Marina's wedding presents. The little Shakespeare statuette takes me back in memory to Munich in the 1930s when Elizabeth Paget (after von Hofmannsthal) was given seats by the director, and used to take me to the opera. Together we were at the first performance there of *Arabella*, conducted by Strauss himself.

Always at hand, on the desk, is a little volume of poems, annotated by Maud Russell, a life-long friend, and given to me by her son Martin after her death. It was Maud who took me to hear Toscanini's *Falstaff* in Salzburg in 1934 – certainly one of the greatest and most memorable operatic performances of this century.

In flowerpots grows a little cress with tiny pale mauve daisy-like flowers which I brought back as a cutting from Mishkenot in Jerusalem – the enchanting ex-Montefiore house that is now used to house the cultured guests who have been invited by Teddy Kollek to visit the city, of which he is the much-loved mayor.

A flower vase was given to me by the student who had made it at the art and craft school in Isfahan when I lectured there in the sixties. A beeswax candle from Hilandari Monastery on Athos that I still light every day I am in the house has a brass 'stick' mounted on a large cowrie shell that belonged to Raymond Mortimer.

Then there are memories of journeys taken to photograph Islamic architectural sites for the two books that Faber & Faber published. A sixteenth- or seventeenth-century tile from Meshed given by the owner of the tile factory on the Gauhar Shad Mosque's roof rests on a bookshelf adjacent to a Moghul watercolour I found in India when painting Rada Krishan, the then president.

The leather, brass-trimmed family chair that had belonged to my grandfather is in front of curtains made of material brought from India, and the William Morris 'tapestry' dragon curtains once belonged to John Bryson, a Balliol don and previous sitter of mine who was a well-known collector friend of the family. My brother John was responsible for a stencil of feathers in a vase – an art deco motif he painted and used for patterning white upholstery satin curtains in the early thirties. This watercolour I have had framed and it hangs on a door.

In each room of the house there are 'reminders' for other members of my family – things they still remember as belonging to parents and grandparents – but my room seems to be fuller than any of them, and my brothers and their children tread warily when they wend their way through 'Derek's mess' to the other rooms beyond.

Previous page An old leather-covered family armchair stands
in front of curtains of Indian material
and William Morris 'tapestry' dragon curtains.
Left A crowded little corner.

GERVASE JACKSON-STOPS

NORTHAMPTONSHIRE

Above One of the little alcoves where the owner works.
Overleaf The Menagerie's one extraordinary room, a single cube with a coved ceiling.
Rectangular alcoves and little square lobbies are approached through open arches.

When I first saw my room in 1970 it was filled with mouldy straw, up to the ceiling in some places. The windows were boarded up and none of the original sashes had survived. About three of the wide elm floorboards remained; otherwise you stumbled around between the joists in the areas where there was no straw, in a debris of plaster dust and rubble resting on the brick vault of the cellar below. Soldiers had carved their names all over the walls in both world wars and local youths had recorded their amatory exploits in graphic detail.

What made the room so special was the remains of its spectacular rococo plasterwork, clinging – goodness knows how – to the rotten and worm-eaten oak laths. I had seen the building from the village, nearly a mile away, but it looked gaunt and forbidding against the sun. The loss of the lead half-dome over the central bay window and the little pyramid roofs of the pavilions at either end had robbed it of its eighteenth-century character. High on the ridge above the largely ploughed-up park, with no track leading to it, it sat looking so derelict that I had never thought of going up to take a look. But none of this had deterred an indomitable friend, Kisty Hesketh, who urged me to look at the one great room it contained because, as she said, 'It won't *be* there next year.' I went and saw and was conquered.

The Menagerie had been built by an Earl of Halifax in the 1750s as an 'eyecatcher' in the park of the old Montagu family house which lay in the dip near the village. The house has gone, demolished between the wars, but his serpentine lake and icehouse, a triumphal arch and a temple, remain – all of them, like the Menagerie, designed by the rococo architect and astronomer, mathematician and garden designer, Thomas Wright of Durham. 'An expensive building at the Menagerie' was how Horace Walpole described it in 1763, with Lord Halifax's private zoo behind it, a circular enclosure surrounded by a moat, roughly the area of my present garden, 'very prettily disposed with many basons of gold fish'. Here there were 'many curious birds and beasts', including 'Storks; Raccoons that breed there much . . . a very large Strong Eagle, another with a white head; two hogs from the Havannah with navels on their backs; two uncommon Martins, doves from Guadaloupe . . . a kind of Ermine, sandy with many spots.' The build-ing itself was evidently a dining pavilion, and the cellar still contains a fireplace where the servants would have cooked the food, bringing it upstairs through the doors on the back terrace to serve to the gentry.

What I saw by the dim light filtering through boarded windows and holes in the roof, and what so excited me, was an interior of perfect proportions that was really five rooms in one: a single cube with a coved ceiling and a central bay window overlooking the park, opening into rectangular alcoves either side, and with little square lobbies behind them approached through open arches. Only about half the plasterwork decoration remained, but it was of wonderful quality. Six of the Signs of the Zodiac in the cove (highly appropriate for a menagerie) were still more or less intact: Virgo, Libra and Scorpio surrounded by their autumnal garlands of wheat, pears and grapes; and Sagittarius, Capricorn and Aquarius above the chimneypiece with winter ever-greens – ivy, palms and laurel. Above, in the ceiling, was Father Time in the centre holding his scythe and a snake biting its tail (the symbol of eternity), with the Four Winds at the corners.

The room obsessed my thoughts from that mo-ment. With my long-suffering parents' support I approached the lady who owned this half of the estate and she agreed to part with the Menagerie for a nominal sum, knowing it was the only way to save it. Then our trials and tribulations began. Although we boarded it up, boys from the village got in before work could begin and did much worse damage, throwing up bricks to bring the plaster down. I was literally in tears when I came one day to find half of Father Time missing and two of the Winds, scarcely anything of the remaining garland of musical instru-ments on one side of the bay window, and nothing of Apollo in his sunburst above. A road had to be constructed, water and electricity laid on – and in the room itself every weekend was spent with unfortu-nate family and friends scraping the remains of paint patiently off the existing plasterwork, sifting through the old straw for vital pieces as we bundled it out, and removing the sharp hawthorn twigs packed behind the cove by the original plasterers, and now solid with owl and bat droppings. The dust and filth were indescribable, and I was still unsure how we could restore all that was missing. With a generous grant

from the Historic Buildings Council, a Yorkshire firm, Leonard Stead, began in 1976 to replace all the plaster that could be made from mouldings: cornices, dado rails, skirtings, shutter panels, even a complete Doric column that was missing, and three of the four elaborate architraves that the columns support.

But the real stroke of luck was to find a friend, Christopher Hobbs, a sculptor of genius, who was prepared to re-create all the free-hand decoration that was missing. Used to designing films and exhibitions, making garden statuary and painting, Christopher had never taken on plasterwork like this before, but he proved himself easily the equal of the eighteenth-century *stuccatori*. Two old photographs from the National Monuments Record showed the room much less badly damaged in 1945, and very little pure guesswork was needed, although the medallions of Aries, Cancer and Leo are Christopher's – based on engravings of a Chambers temple at Kew.

During the work, the local piano-tuner turned up with his father-in-law, who had been a shepherd boy on the estate before the First World War. He used to sit in the derelict bay window surveying the field when it rained, and could recall much of what was missing – including one of the festoons of musical instruments flanking the bay, which was unrecorded anywhere else. One thing he was adamant about was 'a book of music – and you could read all the notes'. I thought the score should be the scene from Handel's *Alcina* where the enchantress turns everyone into animals, but my friends were scathing about this idea, and thought it much too esoteric. So instead it became Shirley Temple's 'Animal Crackers in my Soup' – a clue for art historians of the future that everything here is not quite as it seems.

The room appeared to have only two layers of paint on it – an overall stone colour, followed by a pink and grey scheme, which we copied as closely as possible, and which I am convinced is eighteenth-century in origin. Christopher mixed the paints to match an area high up behind the cornice where the light had never reached. The chimneypiece, made of a very hard plaster, was painted to look like porphyry and was probably intended to pick up the dark accents of the 'four fine plaistered Urns bronzed, in alto relievo, representing the animals of the four parts of the World', seen by Horace Walpole. These urns had disappeared long ago, but the four niches looked sadly empty without them and Christopher's final triumph was to make new ones. Each is placed in a niche under the relevant Wind in the ceiling above, and according to the true points of the compass. Such was Thomas Wright's attention to detail that even the little bas-relief trophies of arms above the niches are appropriate: Europe is the only one with guns and muskets; Asia has a Turkish shield with crescent moons; Africa, clubs and bows and arrows; and America a tomahawk.

The original furniture would probably have consisted of dark mahogany chairs, placed against the walls, and only brought out by footmen and set round folding tables when dinner was served, usually about three in the afternoon. To find consoles of the right height and width to flank the chimneypiece seemed impossible, so new tables were made by a talented local carver, Lenny Goff, and decorated with friezes of Noah and his wife leading the animals to the Ark against a porphyry background, painted by Ian Kearney. Lenny also carved some splendid architectural lamps for me: two rusticated obelisks based on a design I had found while researching a *Country Life* article on Britwell Salome, and a replica of Queen Caroline's Monument at Stowe. An old friend, Melissa Wyndham, helped me with upholstery and curtain materials, and other pieces of furniture came from my family, including an eighteenth-century counterpane beautifully embroidered with animals, which covers the big circular table and conceals the dreaded television. The alcoves at each side have daybeds which were used by guests until I recently added on some spare rooms, and the lobbies behind them with doors on to the back terrace have become a tiny reading room and writing room respectively ('rithmetic was never a strong subject).

After nearly eight years I find it hard to think of life without the room. It has grown and grown on me, and I hope I never take it for granted. Watching the changing light on the landscape from my bow window, and the changing seasons, seeing the plasterwork in the white light of snow or by the dying embers of a fire, I can understand Thomas Wright's feeling for magic and his attempt to create a little cosmos where mind and matter, time and space, are contained in a perfect order. In the words of the immortal Emily Dickinson it has become 'only a shrine, but mine'.

THE VISCOUNT LAMBTON

ITALY

When I sat down to write this article I was immediately struck by the idea that I was about to write a lot of lies, as I am sure this sitting-room is not 'my room'. Let me explain: there are two kinds of houses, one in which only men live and one in which a woman and children share. A Grand Canyon runs between the two – in bachelor establishments order reigns and ornaments remain unmoved, in mixed houses they don't. For instance, in the room I am describing in this house we have visits from twenty children and grandchildren, consequently disorder reigns for long periods of the year. This makes the two types incompatible. I thought this distinctly when I saw pictures of the late Geoffrey Bennison's sitting-room, which could never have survived children and grandchildren.

The second point is that no drawing-room in any house other than a bachelor's can be said to be a man's room, because women have an effective way of dealing with suggestions. They agree with you then do what they want, so what a man thinks is his room is often not, but he is allowed to pretend it is. Nevertheless, there is one room, especially in English households, where men are able to have their way without much contention and that is the library, where books are the predominant feature and the allies of the male occupant, joining him in opposing change.

My first insistence, which I always personally ensure is carried out, is that a room must be rather untidy with signs of life. I always leave letters where I open them; I know exactly where they are until they are moved, after which I never see them again. I like to have a mah-jong set for it is a beautiful thing, although, thank God, I can't play mah-jong. I like to have backgammon because I have noticed if people don't play bridge they play backgammon and it is a game which can be watched with pleasure, unlike the former. I like the table covered with Claire's photograph books because it is nice to see friends sitting for hours with a happy look on their faces gazing contentedly at photographs of themselves. I like to have strange books and maps and bizarre boxes – I have one of an eye which has looked at me for thirty years. I like to have reference books and dictionaries because it is quite astonishing how often other people don't know what a word means and when I am asked I usually haven't the faintest idea either.

Neither can I bear to have a room without dogs, which is lucky as Claire always collects them, believing them lost waifs even if one of them is fat, sleek and happily walking down a road. We have at the moment seven, and it would have been eight if one hadn't been reclaimed by an irate owner. I don't even mind being bitten, as I can hardly remember a year of my life when a dog hasn't bitten me. I must admit that Tuscan dogs are especially fierce – one sent me to hospital this year – and now I usually carry a heavy stick to hit them on the head with when they get particularly unpleasant.

I also cannot bear a room without books. The pianolo has on its top a set of Dent's *Medieval Cities*, and every table, unless it has been tidied, usually has something on it you can pick up and read. I also insisted the room should be comfortable with big sofas; I cannot talk unless I am sitting down. And the next essential was to have a permanently placed card table on which I can play patience, and what is more, it must be topped with velveteen and be accompanied by four folding chairs covered with the same stuff, as in the whole of my life I have never lived in a house which has not had one of these sets, made by Fortnum & Mason in the 1930s. There is something sensual in playing on velveteen; it caresses you and the softness of the fabric makes it a pleasure to pick up even a bad hand. And then patience is a wonderful solace. Nothing is pleasanter than playing while people talk. I feel no stimulus to challenge or contradict the contentious or bombastic, but sit quietly concentrating on the cards, as if the conversation is interesting I can forget the game, listen, and still automatically play on. This habit puts me at ease; I cannot imagine life without this distraction.

As to the rest of the room, I like it furnished with English furniture. I always think there is something slightly vulgar about French 'pieces'. Even the best of them shine like polished shoes, and I cannot help thinking, for all his good taste and sun kingliness, that there was something vulgar about Louis Quatorze and indeed all the Bourbon furnishings; and I am not surprised they appealed to the newly accepted Rothschilds as they look as if they had been made by them anyhow but that is, of course, an extremely narrow and English point of view.

Since living in Italy I have changed my mind about religious works of art, which I used to consider gloomy. But how could I not in a country where the aristocracy are the most irreligious people in Europe, and it is ironic that this country, birthplace of the Catholic Church, should now be the home of custom without belief. If you live among people who can look with pleasure on a crucifix with Christ nailed up and the Virgin and John wailing about below and feel less moved than we do at a Stubbs picture of a fight between a lion and a horse, how can you take the subject matter seriously as, after all, artists did not choose the straitjacket they were confined in by dogma. I think this can only be realized by those who have lived in Italy for a long time, which makes it difficult for the casual visitor to understand life here. But on the other hand, I feel Italians don't like this room and think it too comfortable, but I like it as I am not demanding – all I wish is to have things around me I know and like, and to be able to sit down comfortably when I wish to read or play patience when visitors start talking.

Previous page Part of the groined ceiling. One of the big sofas considered essential forms a central feature of the room.
Right A still-life detail of pretty objects on one of a pair of gilt- and marble-topped tables.

84

JAMES LEES-MILNE

BATH

Luckily for me my favourite room was there already. I say *luckily* because I have very few ideas of my own, little imagination and not a clue how to 'decorate' a room. I can criticize all right. I know what is in good and what in ghastly taste. I am able to scrap what is unseemly and suggest improvements. I can arrange a room rather well. At least I think so. Alvilde has the imagination and ability.

Just over ten years ago we were obliged to leave the house and garden we both loved. It was sad because when I moved into my spacious bedroom with the vast four-poster I looked forward to dying in it. This was not to be. Such a disappointment.

Not wishing to move far away we bought what is termed a maisonette (apparently a flat has but one floor) in Bath. The agent in showing us round opened a double mahogany door, and there was my library! Immediately I was smitten as by a *coup de foudre*. For a year we inhabited the maisonette and hated it. Alvilde hated it more than I did because there was no garden to speak of. In my selfish way I took possession of the library in which to put those of my books which I had not sold on leaving our previous house. In other words I appropriated the only decent room. Later we were fortunate enough to rent a small house in Badminton village where we now live.

We have kept the library and one back room in the Bath maisonette. I commute on weekdays as regular as clockwork, having the ingrained habits of a cart-horse. I like working to rule, in harness as it were, away from home.

Now I must explain that my library is part of three Georgian terrace houses which William Beckford, late of Fonthill Abbey, bought in 1823, joined together, and inhabited in great style, surrounded by works of art second to none in the history of art collections. He remained here until his death in 1844 at the age of eight-four. Curiously enough the library, which was constructed for him in the mid 1830s by a local architect, H. E. Goodridge, is the only room in the three houses which remains intact.

This I can confirm from a detailed description given by a visitor to Mr Beckford's residence in 1838. It was the lesser library of the establishment, the larger one having been in the house next door. Mr Beckford loved it however, called it his *Grecian Library* – why I cannot imagine – and spent the greater part of his remaining years in it, reading, scribbling scurrilous comments on the endpapers of his books about their authors, and recollecting nostalgically his inglorious past. His presence, I may add, is keenly felt by me. It is my belief that presences of the dead, or ghosts if you will, can only survive in rooms which have not been structurally tampered with and redecorated, as is the case here. Others maintain that ghosts are allergic to electricity, telephones and hot water pipes.

On opening one of the double doors you step into what is, I submit, a rather beautiful room of its kind and date. It is a bit too long and narrow to be perfectly proportioned, and is lit by a pair of windows at the far end, facing south-west. This means that I have to keep the brown holland blinds pulled down, adjusted according to the density of light. Thus is conveyed what Horace Walpole called 'a Gothick gloomth' which suits my splenetic temperament. The library is always crepuscular. The two long sides of the room are lined with Mr Beckford's fitted bookcases of red mahogany veneer over walnut. Below them are cupboards and drawers for the ponderous folios of his rare engravings. Shelves and cupboards are divided by scagliola pilasters of imitation *giallo antico*. Above a prominent mould of egg and tongue in gold are arched recesses. The arches are painted to resemble the scagliola of the pilasters which support them. Within the recesses Mr Beckford had Etruscan vases. I only have one such – actually it is Greek of the fourth century BC, if genuine – which, alas, was just too large to fit inside a central recess. So I put it on a black wooden plinth inside the fireplace which, being blocked up, no longer functions. The fireplace is a strange piece of architecture, being made of Devonshire marble, a rather heavy composition jammed between two pilasters. I have grown to like it. Over the chimneypiece is a tall inset mirror under a rounded head.

Let me return to the arched recesses. They are now filled with a pair of carved marble urns – we like to think one is Roman and the other an Italian Renaissance copy – and plaster library busts of Shakespeare, Newton, Milton & Company. Over the doorway I have a marble bust of Byron, and nearby a small one of Shelley which belonged to his grandson. The poet's Victorian daughter was obliged to disown him for being an atheist, and not respectable.

To mitigate the sepulchral 'gloomth' a pair of inset mirrors on either side of the entrance doors, placed opposite the windows, reflect what light I allow. On the shelf in front of each is a pair of large blue-and-white Savona jars with handles and lids, dated 1725. Being of pottery, every time they are dusted pieces flake off. A letter from Mr Beckford to his bankers and a few other trivial treasures – locks of Byron's and Dickens's hair and the fragment of a lovely painted satin dress, dated 1770, of a great-something-grandmother, which I lent to the Bath costume museum – repose under glass.

I think the plain wooden curtain boxes may date from Mr Beckford's time. The yellow curtains with tasselled fringes were chosen by Alvilde and, when drawn, give splashes as of warm sunlight. Between the windows is a coin cabinet which belonged to Mr Beckford. For someone who bought the most exquisite furniture that was made for Marie Antoinette and is now in the Wallace Collection to have designed this hideous little object of yellow varnished oak and ebony, is surprising. Above it hangs in a maplewood frame an unfinished needlework panel of parakeets and mice, done by a great-aunt in 1820. Between the bookcases and the ceiling which is 'belted across and enriched with bands of Grecian tracery in relief', to quote the visitor of 1838, are four indifferent portraits of my Welsh and Scotch forebears. They mean nothing to anybody but me because I know who these dim people were; and am fond of them. On the whole I prefer the dead to the living, and things to people. This is an un-Christianlike admission of which I ought to feel ashamed. But I don't. I adore my possessions. The reasons may be that I have so few and these few are comparatively valueless. If I were the owner of Chatsworth I would probably care less for the world-famous treasures of that gorgeous palace than I do for my modest trash.

As for my books I simply worship them. I am not a bibliophile and have no rare books, apart from a handful which belonged to Mr Beckford and which I like to think may in his day have reposed upon my shelves. One of the things I most regret is having been obliged at certain crises of my life to part with volumes. I simply have to be surrounded by books of reference. After all, they consist of the profoundest thoughts and most beautiful words of the greatest men and women of the world encapsulated within one's reach. They are the most necessary things in life. They *are* life itself.

Malcolm Davidson found for me a very suitable cut glass and ormolu dish lamp, with glass shade and smoke protector, which hangs from the centre of the ceiling. It resembles those depicted in the well-known painting of Lord and Lady Holland seated in the Holland House library. The furniture, however, is sparse because only chairs can go in front of the bookcases. I have a William and Adelaide sofa, hard, upright and uncomfortable, upon which I have been known to recline like St Teresa on her bed of logs. My writing-table in front of the windows is 1890ish Louis Seize. It was bought by Alvilde in France and so exactly resembles the one in a photograph of Monet's drawing-room that I pretend it belonged to him. Beside it is the much-chewed basket in which our whippets repose when they deign to accompany me here. They are extremely tolerant and only interrupt me at stated times. As soon as the clock strikes twelve (not eleven, for they seem to be able to count) they rise to their feet and demand their dinner. Similarly at 3 o'clock they walk to the door and demand a short walk. This can be inconvenient but I solace myself with the thought how far, far more tiresome two fidgety children would be. Thank God I haven't got any. The huge coral-coloured Khorassan carpet was lent to me for my life by Dame Joan Evans.

In the lobby to the library – much too small to swing a cat in – I have an oil sketch purporting to be of Mr Beckford. But as most of my swans turn out to be geese it probably is not. He looks extremely supercilious and disapproving. I am not quite sure how much he likes having me here. At times he makes me feel an interloper. But he has got to put up with me for a little longer. Meanwhile my library is my private retreat to which human visitors are admitted on sufferance.

Previous page Behind the writing-table heavy yellow curtains
with deep pelmets frame the windows.
Above What William Beckford called his 'Grecian' library,
designed for him by H. E. Goodrich in the 1830s. The pilasters of
yellow scagliola support arches of plaster. The curiously cramped
fireplace is of Devonshire marble. Within the recesses
are plaster busts of Milton and Newton.

PATRICK LEIGH FERMOR

GREECE

Left The floor is paved with unpolished rectangles of grey-green stone from Mount Pelion.
The bookcases between the windows are sunk flush with the masonry.
Above Beyond one of the eight thick arches the author enjoys a book and a glass of wine.

The huge fireplace based on a design brought back long ago from Persia. The vertical cone soars towards the wooden ceiling.

'Where a man's Eleventh Edition of the *Encyclopaedia Britannica* is, there shall his heart be also'; and, of course, Lemprière, Fowler, Brewer, Liddell and Scott, Dr Smith, Harrap and Larousse and a battery of atlases, bibles, concordances, Loeb classics, Pléiade editions, Oxford Companions and Cambridge histories; anthologies and books on painting, sculpture, architecture, birds, beasts, reptiles, fishes and trees; for if one is settling in the wilds, a dozen reference shelves is the minimum, and they must be near the dinner table where arguments spring up which have to be settled then or never.

This being so, two roles for the chief room in a still unbuilt house were clear from the start.

*

Twenty-two years ago, when we were the only strangers in the Mani, it was possible to build a house for very little. But it was a challenge. Our headland jutted between a bay and a small cove and there was nothing on it but olive terraces, thistles, asphodels and an occasional tortoise, and here we pitched our tents exactly where the chief room was to be.* There was rock for building everywhere; the friendly and excellent workmen were stonecutters to a man; the occasional visits of an architect friend from Athens helped us with stresses and strains; and we found a brilliant master-mason in the mountain village above

* I tried to write while the building was going up, but, in the war of gerunds, the *furor aedificandi* always triumphs over the *cacoëthes scribendi*, and so it did here.

The many sash windows let in the winter sunbeams.
The ceiling is made of wooden lozenge panels.

– the last of seven generations of master-builders who all played the violin – and prudently became relatives by standing godparents to his small son. Ideas abounded, but it was while it was actually taking shape that we decided how the house should be. In the end, all our mugging up and our drawings and pacings and fiery arguments brought – or so it seemed to us – splendid results.

In two years the house was standing, and because of the rough-hewn, fast-weathering limestone – all prised out of the Taygetus range in whose foothills we live – it looked like a monastery which had been crumbling there for centuries. A wing shot out over the drop of the terraces, outside staircases went up, and the whole thing was roofed over with faded tiles that we picked up for almost nothing, like carrion crows, after the earthquakes in the central Peloponnese.

A gallery of eight thick arches now leads to the room which is our theme. To foil the heat in summer, the walls are nearly a metre thick and the main part of the room measures ten metres by five and a half. You enter from the east along the gallery through the leaves of a heavy beech door. This is framed in a massive bolection of russet stone that we rashly designed without books: the moulding is a foot wide and the torus rises seven inches from the scotia. (There was no road, and except for heavy items, every stick came by mule; but the six-foot lintel of this doorway took twelve men and a ladder and we were sweating and tottering under it when an artless goatherd among the olives asked where we were taking it. 'To the sea,' our godbrother said between his teeth, 'to chuck it in, just in case it floats.') When it was up, we were awed by the mad splendour; it went to our heads and set the pace for all the rest. The long wall opposite was pierced by a French window with a heavy stone beam for a lintel, and above this we put an old marble slab from Paros, perforated by an oval holding a star. This door and the two tall casement windows on either side of it are sunk in elliptically topped embrasures flared through the thickness of the wall, and the grey louvred shutters the other side throw striped shadows over the flag-stones indoors. Spaced out between these three openings and the two similar windows in the north wall, bookcases the same height are sunk flush with the masonry, forming a balancing symmetry of rectangles.

On the same side as the big door we put up a huge fireplace from a design brought back long ago from Persia by a Rumanian friend: a pointed and scalloped arch in a salient bow of honey-coloured ashlars which ends in a vertically bisected cone, whitewashed in the village style, like all the walls indoors; this soars tapering to a wide cornice, and the cornice surrounds a wooden ceiling; both of these are only pine, but twenty years have given them a patina like cypress-wood or cedar. Bars divide the ceiling up into an infinity of squares which recede in vistas and, by a stroke of luck, these and the shape of the room are as acoustically right for music as the inside of a 'cello. The floor is paved with rugous unpolished rectangles of grey-green stone quarried from Mt Pelion and, in the middle, a large intricate star of purple marble bordered with white pulls the whole thing to-gether.

A divan runs all round the north end of the room. Like the long sofa by the fire, it is covered in white linen woven in Arachova. Widened still more by a ledge along the back, this looks very handsome but it makes the shelves there harder to reach; papers, dictionaries, shears and secateurs clutter the ledges and books get lost there for weeks. The bookcases with no divan in front rise nine feet from the floor, and we have discovered a brilliant way of reaching the upper shelves without steps, viz, an 'elephant-pole' of brass-bound teak made by the Hong Kong Chinese to help minor rajahs climb into their howdahs: it splits down the middle and half the pole drops away parallel

with a heartening bang like grounded arms; the rungs, slotted and hinged in hidden grooves, fall horizontal, forming a ladder, and up one goes.

*

But at the end-wall facing south, everything changes. A central opening runs across three-quarters of it, with a coffered soffit along the top a metre thick and the same height as the other lintels, supported at either end by a disengaged hexagonal pillar. You go through, and down a step, into something which, throughout the Levant, is called a *hayáti*. This is a Byzantino-Ottoman winter-chamber, jutting two or three metres from the main room, with low tables and a divan all round. From the wide ledge behind the divan-back spring eight flat grooved wooden columns five feet high – two each side, four in front, rather like the poop of a galleon – and the sash-windows between them, more glass than wall, let in the winter sun-beams through nearly 200 panes. Above, a heavily moulded wooden cornice encloses a lower ceiling than the one in the main room and cut up into lozenges instead of squares to mark the difference. It can become a cavern of shade and perfect for a wildcat snooze in summer by drawing curtains of mattress-ticking, with the stripes running horizontal. In win-ter, rugs cover the wooden floor of this miniature Hardwick (but secret plans are afoot for a Cosmati floor with roundels of porphyry and serpentine edged with bands of black-and-white zig-zag looped together in interlocking figures of eight; perhaps next year . . .). The stone flags of the big room are covered in winter too; near the fire, with *flokkáto* rugs of shaggy goats' hair from Epirus; and kilims from Konia, Smyrna and Ak-Shehir, with light-hearted flower- and geometric patterns of blue, green, white, ochre and orange, strew the rest of the room and give it the look of an Emir's tent.

*

Writing-tables near the French window and behind the sofa, and occasional things here and there like faded William Morris armchairs, strike an English note. The fireplace wall to the east we left free for pictures: two large Japanese seventeenth-century paintings of young goshawks jessed in blue and crimson; Jamaican foliage by Lucian Freud; some Craxton goats; a semi-geometric roof-scape and a design of plants by Ghika, three small Edward Lear Cretan scenes and a Robin Ironside of a recumbent statue waking up in a museum. A Javanese tufa bust of Shiva Mahadeva, and odd fragments of sculpture, are scattered about the divan ledge, and two marble legs stand trunkless beside a marble tree-stump which the vanished god or shepherd must have leant on; they were dug up near Palestrina at the same time as a headless Cybele in a niche in the gallery.

A visiting friend unsettlingly hinted that a Victorian mahogany dining-table – near the *hayáti*-end, and the reference shelves – was not up to the rest; so, years later, we exorcized the complex with an inlaid marble table made by Dame Freya Stark's *marmista* in Venice. Based on a *tondo* in the chancel of S. Anastasia in Verona, white flames of Udine stone radiate from the centre of a design of subtle grey carsico and *rosso di Verona*. When it arrived at last, lugging the triple plinth of Istrian stone down from the road and then trundling the heavy circular top through the trees was as bad as the struggles with the lintel. But the friend was right. Here it is, beautiful and immovable for ever, and when set about with glasses and candles, it turns the humblest meal – even oil and lentils – into a Veronese banquet.

The east door, then, looks out on a row of arches; the north windows, on a green thought in a green shade – cypresses and olive trees, that is to say, and clipped rosemary hedges; and to the south, charmed magic sash-windows open on the foam of, first descending tree-tops, and then the sea. But the axis of the room – and thus of the whole house – is planned so that the west windows, winter and summer, may catch sunset till the last gasp. The terrace outside is a continuation of the room; from the French window you go down two semi-circular steps to a square of terracotta tiles, successfully fired in a local kiln after many attempts. Stone seats girdle the olives here and rings of pebble-mosaic surround them with garlands, wave-patterns, wreaths and cables; then, beyond a low fountain with Seldjuk affinities, the terrace ends in a sort of exedra-like outdoor *hayáti* near the cliff's edge; you go down two steps more to a geometric pebble-patterned rectangle with a big stone table – once a marble balcony and bought for a fiver from a house-breaker in Tripoli – where we feast at night in summer. There are solemn clumps of cypresses on either side of this, and looking from the drawing-room, one's eye shoots on between them, over the cove, past a theatrically placed island and a succession of dragon-capes and across the whole Messenian Gulf to where the sun goes down and the mountains of the Morea rumble away to the north.

*

The room and its offshoots sound grander than they are; but from the stern Mitford test – 'All nice rooms are a bit shabby' – the place comes out with flying colours; time, wear, and four-footed fellow-inmates – born downholsterers and interior desecrators – have put the place out of all danger. Luckily decent proportions (worked out in our tents from Vitruvius and Palladio) and rough building materials have the knack of swallowing up disorder and incongruity. Occasionally a far-wandering hen, hopelessly out of place in a smarter room, stalks jerkily indoors, peers round, stalks out again and all is well. Last month a white goat ventured in from the terrace, soon followed by six more in single file; they trooped clanking across the floor looking as much at home as Jamshyd's lions and lizards, then out along the gallery, down twenty steps and into the landscape again without the goats or the house seeming in any way out of countenance.

But the great advantage of a long room is that different pursuits can go on without impinging: reading, music, letter-writing, talk by the fire, eyelids closing in the *hayáti*: or chess at one end of the room and friends' children on the floor with tiddlywinks at the other; and every seventh of November, which is the Feast of SS. Michael and Gabriel – and also my name-day (*Miháli*, in Greek) – the room fills a special role. These Archangels have a minute chapel three fields away, and after the yearly Mass, a swarm of village-friends, sometimes fifty or sixty, led by the bearded vicar with his bun and stove-pipe hat, come in for a long chat and drinks and *mézé*. Thanks to the divans – suddenly lined with venerable figures in black coifs – the room can hold them all without too much of a squash, and in spite of the immovable table there is plenty of space left in the middle for dancing; and when, later on, the complicated steps of the *syrtos* and the *kalamantiano*, accompanied by clapping and singing, begin to weave their nimble circles round the central star, the room seems to have come into its own at last.

EDWARD MILLINGTON-DRAKE

ITALY

The first time I saw this room was on a foggy November day twelve years ago. There were no window frames. Only the front door, which stood open, remained. There was a gaping hole in the middle of the floor. The house had been advertised in a Roman paper; I was leaving for India the following week and had to decide quickly. I knew little about Tuscany, and had been looking for a house near Rome, but in spite of the bad condition of the building I was immediately captivated by its proportions. I saw at once that the huge barn could become a studio. The wooded hillsides and the complete silence, so rare in Italy, were an added attraction.

Tuscan farmhouses of the type that exist today originated in the eighteenth century, when the Grand Duke gave permission for the conversion of disused defence towers no longer needed to ward off invading armies from France or neighbouring states. Stables, pigsties and sheds, built of stone, were added as the need arose, and later houses were built to a similar model.

This particular farmhouse or *casa colonica* had been abandoned twenty years earlier by tenant farmers, when the post-war economic boom attracted the younger generation away from the land; they were glad to leave the discomfort of houses without electricity or running water, and a system of *mezzadria* which no longer provided a living for a family.

An outside staircase led up to a loggia which opened on to the central room of the house. This was used as both a kitchen and a living-room where the family sat around the only fireplace on wet days or in the evenings. The bedrooms opened off this room, and a wooden staircase led up to a loft for drying olives, and a tower room for storage and breeding pigeons. Below were the stables for oxen, cows and sheep, and, across a small courtyard, a pigsty and the bread oven.

I spent a year supervising the reconstruction of the house to plans drawn up by John Stefanidis, the London designer. The loft in the kitchen was removed to make the ceiling higher, so freeing the staircase to the tower, which became a library. A stone sink was moved to the landing above a new inside staircase which was needed to connect the two floors of the house, and new handmade terracotta tiles were laid to fill in the hole in the floor. A new kitchen was built between the house and the pigsty, and bathrooms and heating were installed.

There are three kinds of possessions: those that are inherited, those bought from necessity such as chairs, tables and beds, and those bought from choice which may serve as reminders of places once visited. Nothing inherited from my family would have looked right in the house except for a few things from a house in Cyprus belonging to my sister. Our furniture was too English, and a Lazlo portrait would have looked out of place in a Tuscan farmhouse. The simple rustic lines of the house limited the choice of furniture; John Stefanidis decided to use comfortable modern sofas and to have chairs, tables and four-poster beds made by the local carpenter.

Looking through books on early Italian art, I notice that there was a definite oriental influence in the decoration of the rooms and buildings in the paintings, similar to those in the cathedrals of Siena and Pisa: there are no carpets on the floor but they appear on tables in Pinturicchio's frescos in the Piccolomini library in Siena. The floors often had geometric patterns in stone or marble, which might be found in Istanbul or North Africa. Ships returning to Pisa and Leghorn must have been loaded with oriental objects and carpets bought or looted on trips around the eastern Mediterranean.

Since the age of twenty-one when I went to Persia to paint for my first exhibition in Paris I have collected objects and fabrics wherever I went. In this room there are silver bowls and wooden boxes from Ladakh, a head of Christ from Goa and a brass chest from Tripoli. John Stefanidis decided that curtains would make the rooms dark, and to compensate for the coldness of bare whitewashed walls he used south Indian fabrics as bed curtains and ikats from Java to cover the seventeenth-century Italian chairs. Other Javanese fabrics are used in the room on sofas, and one hangs from the banister; the cushions are covered in Rajasthan cottons. Their simple designs and natural dyes blend well with the Caucasian kelims and ivory inlaid tables and chest.

After the last war, when paint was expensive, farmers in Italy used anti-rust on doors and windows which faded to a pale pink, now no longer to be seen. This gave me the idea of painting the windows and some of the doors pale pink, which helped to lighten the rooms. John Stefanidis told the painter to put a little ochre in the whitewash to soften the whiteness which in winter can be depressing. My house in Patmos is rather similar and has whitewashed walls and tiled floors; there too are brass chests, kelims and inlaid Indian furniture, but in Greece the walls, sofas, cushions and bed curtains are all white. The constantly changing shadows in the rooms in daytime and differing shades of blue on the walls defy the use of other colours.

Hanging pictures in a new house is always difficult. Bare walls are forbidding, and paintings and drawings on whitewashed walls often do not look right. I see so much of my own work in the studio that I was not anxious to hang many pictures. Nevertheless the colours, texture and motif of one of the abstract paintings I was doing at the time went so well with the room that it was hung on the north wall; but the other walls are bare except for a large carved Tuscan mirror, the reflection of which gives additional volume to this long room. Windows in Tuscany are small, to keep out the cold in winter, but this room has a large north window with a brick pediment, a curious architectural feature of which there are many to be found in the region. In the evenings when I am alone I open the doors of all the rooms and turn on the lights to make the room seem larger and because I like views of rooms through doorways.

This room, like the studio and much of the furniture in the house, is unrelated in many ways to its Tuscan surroundings. Predominantly they reflect my love of India and the East, where I have worked and travelled so extensively. My house is that of an expatriate – I have lived abroad for thirty years – but my nostalgia is not for 'home' but for the East. The pigeons cooing in the early morning remind me of my room on the lake in Udaipur, and my dogs were born in a monastery in western Tibet. When I look at the woods, brown in the winter as in Rajasthan, it is India I think of more than Tuscany.

Previous page The loft above the old kitchen was removed in order to heighten the ceiling. Large, comfortable sofas covered in white contrast with the abundance of oriental materials.
Right Another aspect of the room that has been so cleverly converted.

DAVID MLINARIC

LONDON

Sepia-wash views of ancient sites of Britain.

My family lives in a studio house in Chelsea. There are only a few of them, and we have been lucky enough to live in two, one after the other. I have nearly always had a room, flat or house in Chelsea and, until recently, lived and worked in the same place. This studio was more for working in, but the balance has changed. It is now in fact a bed-sitting-room for my wife and myself. We sleep on the gallery, which we built a few years ago, and live in the room below. It is large by London standards and we have tried to arrange it to be as agreeable as possible with either two or twenty people in it. It is the largest room in the house and our children like to play in it, so it has no distinct single purpose.

People who come to see me here for the first time for work react differently to what they see. Some seem to have been expecting something more showy; others find it easy and are pleased with the economy with which the effects are built up. Sometimes they are relieved that it is not intimidating; others seem disappointed, as they seem to expect an interior decorator to live in more splendour.

A room which a decorator makes for himself is bound to reflect his views in the context of time. In the future when people look back on English decoration of the second half of the twentieth century, I think a dominant thread will appear to be the continuous and varied re-working of elements of the past. This will be seen in contrast to the eighteenth and nineteenth centuries when the new was what was wanted. In the first half of this century the new way was, as always, exciting. It was more fashionable too than it is in the second half. In spite of the post-war modern style, what we still seem to like a lot at home are revivals or versions of what could be seen in their original context until the First, and even the Second World War. This is partly for nostalgic reasons and partly because there has been so much of the past to digest and work through.

Every few years there has been an enthusiasm for a period style re-found and made popular again. Since the last war there have been, among others, Regency, Victorian, art nouveau, art deco and fifties. Even some of the look of the sixties is now re-emerging. However, one of the strongest in the last twenty years has been for the bolder visual aspects of eighteenth-century England. Not the neo-classic Jane Austen atmosphere of the silk hung drawing-room with gilded furniture which, like classic French decoration, has never been unpopular. It has been more for heavier masculine furniture; large in scale, strong in character, sometimes Irish. Large dark paintings and the contents of top floors and back stairs have been looked at again. The nineteenth-century character of libraries and clubs, life below stairs, even the look of the headmaster's study has been picked through and borrowed from.

Now, because of the great increase in value of antiques and objects of the past, they are becoming further out of reach for all but a few people. This, combined with the fact that there will soon be nothing else to revive, suggests that a more widespread sophisticated modern style is becoming urgently needed.

This house was built in about 1880 and would have been thought up to date when it was new. It was planned to suit both living and working together and has a number of details which fit in with the old rules of building, where everything had its proper place. If one looks into them, these rules are as complicated as those which controlled speech, dress and behaviour. They are often based on status. It is as if a visual code was worked out to inform the observer at a glance where he had come to and what he was looking at. The character here is somewhere between a normal domestic house and a commercial building of the same date, and this is visible in the architectural detail. There are bare walls outside; red brick and tuck pointed on the front, plain London stock on the back. Inside there are cornices in the front rooms but not the back. The front door is panelled, the back door merely beaded. The house has a character and a status of its own, with subtle relationships to other buildings of its date.

When this is seen to be the case, it is usually best for the decorations and interior arrangement to answer the questions put by the architecture. Except in rooms of fantasy and spectacle it is better to show inside what you expect or hope to find from looking at the outside. In this house it would be a disappointment not to find moulded joinery, fireplaces, rooflights, tiled kitchens and bathrooms. In the rearranging, details were therefore borrowed, for example, from the staircase when the gallery was built, and a conservatory was made over the previous back yard in the manner of the window glazing bars.

Each time something is added, whether an

architectural feature or a piece of furniture, a change takes place to the space and light of the room. This room has come to its present form by growing, rather like a garden. There has been coaxing, weeding out, transplanting rather than a master plan being followed. Some things have been here a long time, others are new. A lot have been removed for being too big, too small or for not showing their best. Some things are given key positions, some are backgrounds, sometimes irrespective of their quality. We have tried to make it agreeable in summer and winter, night and day, full or empty, tidy or in disarray. We have been here for nine years and it has changed quite a bit. It will probably change again, but at present it feels very easy.

Nearly everything in the room is liked by both my wife and myself, as often as not for its associations. The painting above the fireplace is by Rex Whistler and is of my wife's mother and her sister. The painting opposite is of my first studio and the chandelier shown in it is the one hanging in this room. In the shelves, some of the books are from when we were at school, with exam papers still between the pages. A lot of the drawings on the walls are by friends, others made by our children. If we had a more conventional drawing-room I doubt that we could have had such a mix, or felt such freedom in dealing with it. Here it does not matter that the chandelier is too big or that some of the pieces of furniture are so close that they touch.

The characteristic of an English room most envied abroad is its ease. This is as much to do with the attitude of the owner as the style. The dividing line between a pleasure and a burden is in a different place for everyone, but anyone attempting decoration to a standard above average needs to think out how much he is prepared to do. It shows when a house has become an anxiety and its owner tyrannized by the demands of upkeep or security. It shows also when a person is out of context although at home. In the end a good room is one in which one can relax, in which the owner has enhanced what he started with without it looking as if he has taken too much trouble, and in which his choice is controlled by his needs. Where there is no purpose, there is no point.

The big studio room with the recently added gallery, used as a bedroom.

PROFESSOR
BERNARD NEVILL

LONDON

I am essentially an assembler of things. The way rooms come together through rearranging today the ingredients of rooms of other times fascinates me. As in a kaleidoscope the same particles form and re-form, always producing different yet familiar patterns. I dislike the commonplace and have always tried to eschew fashionable attitudes in decoration, preferring mellow, faded, slightly shabby rooms with worn leather armchairs and furnishings which have the harmony and colour bestowed by the kindly hand of time – all curtains throughout my house are antique. Long considered eccentric, this style is now accepted as desirable. I *listen* with my eyes – and sometimes find that having an eye for detail which never rests, constantly weighing up, re-appraising and seeking improvement in the order of things, is at odds with my belief that no room should look too well thought out – an artless unstudied look is what I aim for. I think it is only after forming a friendship with a room that we move with ease and freedom against our chosen backgrounds. My passion for old buildings extends from great castles and half-timbered manor houses to Voysey vernacular rough-cast villas, Webb red-brick and quaint, cosy, Baillie-Scott Sussex cots. In fantasy I possess them all, wandering through their many towers and gables; the wealth of polished floors, gleaming silver and brass, old paintings and china, rare tapestries, and crackling fires delights me. Eagerly entering the spirit of the age I gather them all to me and embrace their various seasonal moods. Through deep-seated casements, stylized Gregory Brown downs, Elgood/Jekyll gardens and terraces, William Robinson woodlands are revealed beyond, accompanied by Gurney and Warlock songs, or Fauré sonatas – all this I love, induced and nourished no doubt by a lifetime's poring over old bound volumes of *Country Life*, Fletcher Moss's *Pilgrimages to Old Homes* and Latham/Tippings's *In English Homes*, where one finds an abundance of the old-world houses and gardens of yesterday, which I strongly respond to.

The large Ziegler carpet, deep-seated Howard sofas and heavy tapestry curtains create a harmonious atmosphere, with light from the large Chelsea Old Rectory garden flooding the end of the room.
Overleaf The Charles Furze portrait of Lady (Ian) Hamilton in her famous Worth cape.

Equally I have many favourite types of English room – idealistic impressions formed early on by a fascination for the turn-of-the-century illustrators Hugh Thompson, Caldicott and Cecil Aldin. Consequently one's view of sixteenth-, seventeenth- and eighteenth-century English interiors has been permanently coloured by seeing them through late nineteenth-century and Edwardian eyes. Helen Allingham's *Happy England*, Margaret Waterfield's evocative country watercolours and T. N. Foulis's books have all been profound and insidious influences. I greatly admire the continuity given to country houses by the accumulation of things gathered together over the centuries, and envy the great age when the wealthy were able to use the architectural knowledge learned on the Grand Tour to rebuild and alter their houses, returning laden with objects to beautify both house and garden. Although I prefer clutter and walls closely covered with pictures, I also like to see – in certain houses – a degree of architectural severity, a restricted use of decoration and the economy of just a few well-placed objects in the manner of Vanbrugh or as seen in backgrounds of early eighteenth-century paintings.

From out of these many jostling images emerges the type of room I most admire – it combines the best elements of a country house library, a long gallery and a gentleman's club, ideally having the proportions and scale of a long gallery with ceiling-high bookcases and massive comfortable furniture – the Reform Club library comes to mind, and I have often thought how splendid and satisfying it would be to have it as one vast magnificent bed-sit. I have always preferred large objects on the grand scale which add a touch of swagger – the diminutive has no place in my personal scheme of things. The ideal time to indulge in acquisition was during the late fifties and early sixties, when many of London's finest clubs – monuments to Victorian and Edwardian opulence and splendour – were demolished; I bought from the Conservative, Constitutional, Bath and Junior Carlton Clubs, also from the New Club, Edinburgh, many architectural fittings, bookcases, marble chimneypieces, ornamental door frames and mahogany doors, massive library tables, leather chesterfields and armchairs and huge Turkey carpets which have ever since formed the most important elements – combined with other inherited pieces and things collected from country house sales – in creating a comfortable, insulated and reassuring background wherever I have lived. Today several of these are placed in my library/drawing-room at West House (Philip Webb, 1869, for the watercolourist G. P. Boyce), waiting until I fully restore Boyce's first-floor studio to its original proportions, when the library will move upstairs. All my previous London homes have been studios, so I am accustomed to living in very large open spaces with top-lit ceilings.

The walls of my present drawing-room are still hung with the not unpleasant pale yellow wallpaper which was here when I moved in. Eventually it will be replaced with a brown gilded leather-type paper richly embossed with vines and pomegranates, salvaged from the Imperial Institute. The vast Ziegler carpet and pair of immense deep-seated Howard sofas – one in the process of being covered gradually with seventeenth- and eighteenth-century *gros-point* fragments – came from a large country house library (Rudding Park). When the Conservative Club bookcases, designed by Henry Whitaker in the 1840s, move upstairs they will regain their heavily moulded oak and bronze cornices – meanwhile insufficient ceiling height dictates their removal – and rejoin the handsome original Connemara marble chimneypiece he designed to run in line. I bought the pair of library ladders when *The Times* demolished their old building – the matching third turned up years later in a Putney second-hand shop, where I identified the owner as the former head porter of the sale . . . My 'Expert' gramophone was a present from Griselda Joynson-Hicks after she closed down the Monkey Club in Mitford House – the girls learnt to type by it, but now it plays vocal and chamber music from my collection of old 78s. Two twelve-foot-high looking-glasses formerly in the Junior Carlton Club, several life-size portraits, and a large unusual painted picture frame – a present from Edward Le Bas – are stacked awaiting a permanent home at Fonthill Abbey. In fact the only object of permanence in this room – made to replace the pelmet board with concealed lights illuminating the ceiling, found on arrival – is the thick mahogany curtain pole, shaped to fit the bay window. Evidence to the power of wish-fulfilment is Charles Furze's life-size, full-length portrait of Lady (Ian) Hamilton in her famous Worth cape. During a visit to Jane Willoughby at Glenartney, I paid sixpence in a Perth bookshop for General Sir Ian Hamilton's charming memoir of his wife, its frontispiece a striking

portrait in colour. I lusted for it, and years later attending the sale at Blair Drummond Castle – there it was at the end of a dark corridor. Of the many pleasures and delights this favoured room bestows, I enjoy crystallizing all the variations in mood and those moments, when sudden unexpected splashes and shafts of sunlight fall on gilt bindings, silver, brass, making glass sparkle, bringing out the sombre sheen of dark bronze statuary and lamps, catching the ormulu festoons of husks and borders which embellish the pair of ebony Pietra Dura cabinets, spotlighting the head in a portrait and causing unusual glimpses of garden, reflected in the glass of a picture frame. Colours are reflected from curtains on to walls and in polished floors. The aspect of the room changes by night. In *Dreamthorpe* Alexander Smith wrote, 'In my garden I spend my days, in my library I spend my nights' – my own sentiments, although it is really in winter as dusk comes, sitting in my library walled round with all the comfort my books and fireside give me, the heavy tapestry curtains drawn, that it's most reposeful and a great joy. As light fades one's eye starts exploring as the room takes on deep melancholic shades seen in old master paintings – I like rooms with a tendency towards darkness – flickering firelight, ticking and chiming clocks complete a state of harmony and emphasize – perhaps the most remarkable quality about West House – the stillness and quiet it possesses through its unique setting overlooking the two-and-a-half-acre Chelsea Old Rectory garden.

The ceiling-high bookcases designed by Henry Whitaker for the Conservative Club, and one of the library ladders acquired when *The Times* demolished their old building.

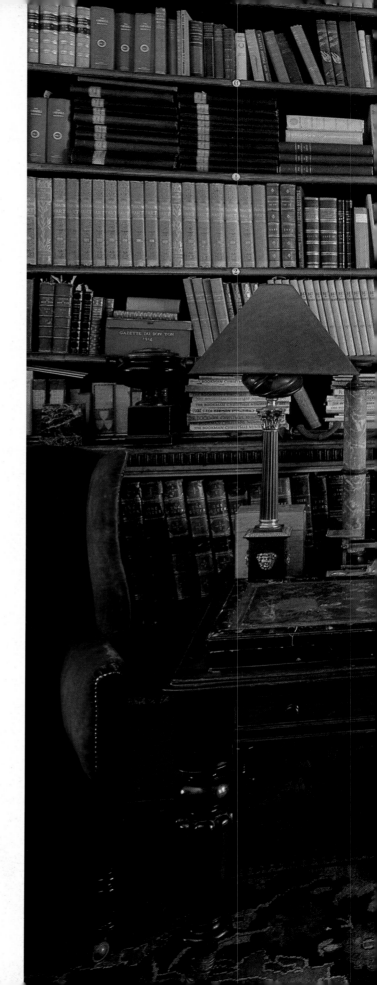

NIGEL NICOLSON

KENT

There are many books about and by the Bloomsburies. Above the fireplace
hangs John Piper's painting of the White Garden, done in 1984.

My writing-room at Sissinghurst is called the Virginia Room, after Virginia Woolf. Not that she ever entered it, or that it would have looked like this if she had, but because it was in this room that I edited her letters, and it contains, on an upper shelf, her bust, a bronze by Stephen Tomlin which he made in 1931. Her impatience while she had to sit for it in his 'rat-ridden and draught-riddled studio' made her so cross that she had no comment to make in her diary or letters about the bust itself, but it would probably have been unfavourable. She detested her appearance, which everyone else envied, but she was undeniably vain and would have thought this profile unflatteringly gaunt.

That's all there is of Virginia in this room, unless you count a steel filing cabinet which contains photocopies of her letters, and a poster from Stanford University, California, advertising a lecture about her. The only other evidence that this is a Bloomsbury room is a painting by Duncan Grant of a water-scene, I think in Venice, and many books by and about the Bloomsberries – a sample of that 'library' which inexplicably infuriates reviewers when yet another book is added to it.

The room, I agree, lacks distinction. The desk at which I spend much of my day comes from a multiple-store in Tunbridge Wells, and I bought it because it was the only one on show that would fit into the back of the car, and I needed it in a hurry for my co-editor of Virginia's letters, Professor Joanne Trautmann, who was about to arrive from Pennsylvania. She sat at it, and I at an oak table which lies at right angles. For six years running, but only in June and July, we occupied this room, tossing diagonally across it questions like: 'What's the difference between passable and passible?'; 'When did the *Titanic* sink?'; 'Will these people be hurt to read that Virginia thought them "on the lowest rung of life, water-blooded, blowsy, grumpy, servile; not a drop of hope or health in them"', or should we put dots for their names?' (We put dots.)

Then there's a heavy oak trough which my father designed to hold reference books at a convenient reach and angle, a fake-Turkish stool on which a visitor can perch, a brand-new tilt-and-swivel chair which is the only smart object in the room, a few electronics like a photo-copier which hasn't worked for six years, a tape-recorder, a toppling angle-poise,

an electric fire, and three telephones, one of which purrs for the National Trust, a second which squeals for me, and a third, cordless, which I can carry round the house. Then the usual apparatus of a writer's room, typewriter, clipper, puncher, things to hold pens and other things to hold stationery. The ceiling-light is interesting. I bought it at St Tropez, thinking it was unobtainable elsewhere (but you can buy it in our local town, Cranbrook), and hoping that children would ask me how it was made, because it is just a globe of string. Almost all of them, disappointingly, know the answer. The string was coated and wound round an inflated balloon, which was then burst and extracted when the string set hard.

I feel a little ashamed of my room. I think it should contain more memorable objects, or at least objects which indicate more formidable a personality. If it belonged to a stranger, I would say, 'Here is a man who is indifferent to his surroundings. Why are there no flowers, when outside his window is one of the loveliest gardens in England? How can he tolerate so unpleasing a desk-lamp, or for that matter, the desk? Why all those ugly box-files? A metal filing cabinet should have no place here. The room is just a throwing-together of ill-selected conveniences.' The stranger might be a little more sympathetic when he examines the books which surround the room on three sides, for they do represent a certain continuity of half-a-dozen interests, and (it is strange that it should be so) serrated lines of multi-coloured bindings and paper-jackets which form a pleasing, warming, accidental but homogeneous pattern against the walls, particularly in a small room.

I like its smallness. It is only four paces in each direction. I feel cocooned by it. It can be warmed by a single electric bar. In summer I hear the footsteps and muted talk of the visiting public outside, but they disturb me no more than the birds and bees. I can look out of the window on a tall Elizabethan tower. My mother Vita used this room during the war when her writing-room in the tower became, even for her, unendurably cold, and perhaps dangerous when the flying-bombs began to fall. Then it became the bedroom of her secretary, Ursula Codrington. Then a miniature estate-office. But that encompasses only forty years of its five centuries (this range was built in 1490, but I tell American visitors 1492), and I have no idea what went on within these four solid walls before then, and I don't much care, because all but its shape is completely changed by the way I have adapted it.

I do not regard it as a particularly private room, and anyone can enter it if I am out, or without knocking if I'm in, for I have not inherited Vita's fiercely defensive attitude towards her tower-room, which I entered only three times during the last thirty-two years of her life, not by explicit prohibition but by an unspoken understanding that it was her sanctum. I suppose that few men guard their privacy to the same degree as women (but the rest of this book may contradict this theory), and as I grow older (or is it old?) I have a diminishing number of secrets to guard. For years I have written a diary in this room, at first daily, now on average weekly, but anyone who knows me could read it without interest or surprise. The same with my bank statements and tax returns, which I keep in an unlocked drawer. But it wasn't for these reasons that Vita barred her tower-room to her family and all but a few close friends. It was because she wanted one room in the house where she need never fear intrusion. My Virginia Room isn't like that. My children come in and out to telephone or explain plans, and most people who come to Sissinghurst to discuss something with me, a new boiler or a university dissertation, find themselves closeted here for anything between a minute and a couple of hours. It is not a room to lounge in. The Turkish stool is an awkward perch, and the only visitor's chair is set behind a table to encourage the idea that talk here is purposeful and terminable. There are more comfortable rooms elsewhere in the house for talk which need be neither. But I will not have the Virginia Room called an office or a study.

One aspect of the room I can explain but not justify. I write with my back to the window. Always I have said that I could not bear to use Vita's tower-room as my own, not only because it was filled with her possessions and personality, but because the windows were too high to see out of them without standing up, and her writing-table faced a wall. In fine weather I often leave the Virginia Room for a gazebo in the garden, where the built-in desk lies beneath a great window looking over the Kentish Weald almost as far as Canterbury, and when people say that it must be very distracting to write facing so beautiful a view, I reply that it is like a glass of champagne – one takes occasional sips. From where I sit in the Virginia Room, I have only the view of three walls and the door. Why not re-place the chair to face the window and the tower? That is what I would prefer, but a primitive sense of caution prevents it. One cannot sit with one's back to the only door, at least not a door which opens immediately behind the chair. Outside there is an uncarpeted back-staircase to the kitchen. I hear, and often recognize, climbing footsteps. I need to confront the arrival face-to-face, and so, I expect, does the arrival.

This is not the sort of room which a decorator would design, and no decorator did or could, for it is shaped by historical accident, furnished for convenience, and its decoration is its books. There are only three works of art in it – the Duncan Grant, the Virginia bust, and above the unused fireplace a view of the White Garden painted in the summer of 1984 by John Piper. Looking around me, I can see several things which I would like to remove, or re-place or tidy before Derry Moore comes to photograph the room, but I felt that this would be cheating, like pretending in *Desert Island Discs* that your musical favourites are more sophisticated than they actually are. The room, I think, illustrates a man of simple but not austere tastes, slightly unadventurous (but what about the cordless telephone?), reasonably well-organized (in-tray, out-tray, files), a bit slothful, reconciled to be who he is, and very content to be where he is.

I believe that the main characteristic of this room is its cosseting intimacy, which may indicate something of its occupant's diffidence. At least, that is how I would see it if I were a stranger to myself. I never thought of the Virginia Room in these terms until invited to describe it. If I left Sissinghurst, which I never shall, I would instinctively choose the smallest room in the new house, apart from a loo, and make it my own.

The room is only four paces in each direction
and creates a 'cosseting intimacy'.

TOM PARR

FRANCE

For many years I have dreamed of the house in the country that one day I should buy. Although the ideas that I had about all the rooms in the house changed often over the years, my original thoughts about the kitchen remained steadfast.

I have never wanted a dining-room. It seems to me to be a waste of a room, and I like to eat in front of the fire in the sitting-room, in the library in front of the television, on the terrace, or in the kitchen.

The space that was originally intended for a dining-room in my new house in France is going to be a library where I can curl up in winter in front of the fire and watch television, or eat while I watch the absorbing antics of Alexis and Krystle dubbed into French!

The vision of the kitchen that I would have one day was always the same; a long large room with at one end an old-fashioned cream Aga, either side of which were two large chintz-covered armchairs on which a number of cats slept and stretched. In the centre of the room, on the old worn stone floor, was a huge scrubbed pine kitchen table on which I envisaged blue and white Liverpool transfer ware plates, loaves of home-made bread, a blue and white jug of milk with a muslin cloth covering it, weighted at the edges with coloured beads, and trugs burgeoning with vegetables newly arrived from the garden ('I've managed to find you enough baby broad beans for dinner, sir').

Now at last I have my country abode, a small neo-classical house in the foothills near Grasse, and here I have made a kitchen dining-room – but since the house is totally unsuitable for the room described above, the resulting room is quite different.

The area which formerly contained a tiny low-ceilinged kitchen, an even smaller pantry, two servants' bedrooms and their bathroom was the restricted canvas on which I was to paint my picture.

The Aga was out of the question, even if only on grounds of the heat that it would generate in the long

The Capo di Monte plates have views of Naples in sepia. The walls are upholstered in fawn-and-white cotton ticking.

hot summers; no large armchairs as the space would not allow it; no cats by order of Miss Elsa de Wolf, my German Shepherd dog, who regards all felines as creatures only to be chased up trees; no kitchen garden as yet to produce vegetables, although the market in Grasse is an unending source of young, scrubbed and manicured vegetables, and fruit, which is to me a great joy – a far cry from the filthy, badly displayed produce that most of our greengrocers offer their uncomplaining customers.

The strange-shaped area with which I was presented, being an unsuitable one in which to realize my grandiose dreams, had to be planned to contain two separate areas, one for cooking and one for eating. I was also left with an extra space which I pretentiously called the 'ante-room'. The dining part seats eight people, and when we are more numerous I put up a table in the ante-room to seat six more people. Furthermore, there is one of several terraces giving off the room, this one facing east, and known as the 'breakfast terrace', where the sound of water from the fountain in the nearby courtyard cools and calms, and where for long periods of the year we have breakfast and sometimes luncheon, and where I have made a raised bed where tarragon, chives, dill, parsley (both *frisé* and Italian) and marjoram grow in profusion, and where there are two large pots of basil and one of bay. All these herbs can be gathered at a moment's notice when they are required.

The planning, therefore, as is usually the case when adapting an old house, was dictated to me by the restrictions of the building, and by my requirements. The decorative scheme was easily decided upon. Some years ago I inherited a wonderful late eighteenth-century Capo di Monte creamware dinner service on which are views of Naples in sepia. This wonderful service came from Fulco Verdura, the great Sicilian jeweller, who in turn inherited it from Cole Porter. I could never find a satisfactory way of displaying it in London, so I decided that this would provide the *'point de départ'* around which I would build the kitchen. I chose the fawn and off white ticking stripe that I used to upholster the walls as a foil to the dinner service and to provide good acoustic properties in the eating part of the room and the ante-room. The dining-table is an old walnut one that

I bought in a local junk shop and the chairs are simulated bamboo sent out, like so much of my furniture, from England. I use various different plates depending on the food being served, and the season. There are countless attractive local pottery ones still being made at Biot and Apt and Vallauris. The floor is made of large terracotta tiles – the French Provençal equivalent of the old stone floor of which I had dreamed so long – and on this, in the dining part of the room, there is a matting rug from neighbouring Cogolin to provide some feeling of warmth in winter, and which I can remove in summer.

All the kitchen units were designed by my colleague Lou Kracmar, and were made by the local carpenter and painted a pale creamy fawn colour; the worktops are of solid teak – no miracle man-made laminate for me. These tops are crowded with gadgets – ice-cream makers to turn the fruits from the ever-growing array of fruit trees that I cultivate into ice creams and sorbets; an orange squeezer with which to prepare delicious juice from those trees that have been spared by this icy winter; an espresso coffee machine without which I would find it hard to live! There is also a space for books, among others the works of Elizabeth David, who has been my mentor for years. Now at last I can buy locally all the ingredients about which she writes with such love.

On the part of the counter that projects into the room, thus dividing the working part of the room from the dining part, are a collection of baskets in which are displayed the results of my latest forays into the food markets – baby artichokes, fennel, radishes and dried sausages, together with peaches, cherries, greengages, apricots and grapes from the garden.

I have always preached to my clients the importance of suitability in designing and decorating a house or room. I feel it is important that the decorative scheme, the choice of furniture and the general layout should help the architecture, and not fight against it, just as it should reflect the function of the room and the geographical position of the house. It was for these reasons that I was forced to abandon my long-dreamt-of kitchen, but while I have had to alter totally my original ideas, the present arrangement gives me enormous pleasure.

Part of a fine eighteenth-century Capo di Monte service
inherited from Fulco Verdura, who in turn inherited it
from Cole Porter.

THE RT HON. J. ENOCH POWELL, MP

LONDON

Here in this rectangle, twelve feet by nine, sit I at my desk surrounded by the compacted strata of seven decades of life. The strata consist, of course, of books. For all my life has been about words: manuscript words, printed words, spoken words. Thinking, loving, fighting, striving have always revolved around words – not mere words, but words, because apart from words men are but as brutes.

When we moved twenty-eight years ago from our first married home into this late Georgian terrace house, the remover, who had underestimated for the books, dumped them in a pyramid on the floor of this, the short arm of the L-shaped room which such Belgravia houses mostly have. As I built shelves against the walls, covering eventually all accessible space from floor to ceiling, I tidied up into them the printed and bound deposits of my previous existence as they came to hand. So upon the whole, by virtue of the sheer inertia which books once on a shelf possess, they have remained and I dare say will remain.

Under the ceiling frieze runs Hansard, complete from the end of the Second War, though only up to the early 1950s. Since then it has bolted, like a Russian vine, into nearly every other room, corridor and staircase in the house. From the remaining shelves great slabs of the past stare out at me, encouragingly or reminiscently, much as a Roman householder must have been stared at by his *lares* and *penates*.

As if to guard my back, where I sit in my working chair, rise rows of worn Greek and Latin classics – my hand would go straight to whomever I wanted – gradually yellowing and ageing with the years and the sunlight. Lucky boy, to have started that collection in the best Greek school in England, though the largest part of the library in my fellow's rooms at Trinity College, Cambridge went back to the college in 1939, as a pessimistically premature legacy marked RIP on the packing cases. I like having the classics close to me, like a warm reassurance that some things can be possessed that nothing takes away afterwards.

The other stacks are somehow not so cosy. There's one there, straight in front of me, with the uncompromising label WAR. Out of the corner of my eye I catch sight of the German edition of Clausewitz, which I bought in Cambridge when an infantry private in 1939, to lay the foundation of the study of what another military philosopher, not Clausewitz, called 'that terrible and impassioned drama'.

Two other blocks, left and right of the window, house the collection of books about India which I greedily acquired along with an interpretership in Urdu during the three years of my love affair with that land in 1943–6. It has grown steadily since, and still grows, but more slowly. A tiny bit of the debris of the British Raj, material and emotional, which time has washed up on the beach of history, is there in those volumes, some with the student's eager manuscript notes, some with cockroach tracks over the covers, others with a munshi's *pan* stains on the pages. The dust gathers on them now: nothing is so closed as a closed book – unless it be a closed era.

Another bookstack started out briskly but optimistically as ECONOMICS. But hold once taken, its contents grew out of all control, higgledy-piggledy, old books, reprints of old books, new books, pamphlets – a Faustian nightmare – until further accretions were banished from this room and consigned to ramble wherever else they could find footage to be piled upon. The original nucleus that remains is a reproachful sort of companion, which insists upon recalling past enthusiasms cooled, past crusades turned to boredom, past convictions under whose banners other champions slay and are slain on the political and intellectual battlefield. A sort of silent cynical whimsy lurks in that corner; my glance is never quite at ease there.

Without any particular reason, the eye falls on to two shelves of me – or rather one shelf of me and one

Previous page and above Statesman and author Enoch Powell in his small
room filled with favourite and much-read books on every subject.
They are carefully arranged under their various titles.

shelf about me. The first group consists of the actual printed and bound 'remains', as they used to call them, from the first in German in a German periodical in 1931 to the last effusions of the 1970s. Not all is there, of course: entombed (ironically) in safes elsewhere are the ephemera, written or spoken, and (fond conceit whispers) are there not indices to those volumes of Hansard, embalming lost hopes and lost causes, under the initial letter P–? The second shelf houses the premature biographies, polemical or studious, including one German doctoral dissertation on Powell's syntax. No, is the answer to the reader's question: not narcissism, but just that one does need the stuff where one can lay hands upon it.

Besides the books there is the bric-à-brac, collecting dust on walls and shelf tops. No system or classification is discernible in it at all. True, every Porson prizeman has a steel-engraving of the Hoppner portrait, and what Tory need apologize for prints of Peel and Disraeli. The remainder just managed to settle wherever at the time there was a bit of vacant space. No jealous rivalries have kept the items apart. Cambridge University is represented and St Andrews too. The Tory front bench of 1881 in Spy's cartoon does not seem to resent the wuzzy oleograph of Gladstone having tea with Mrs on the lawn at Hawarden, which immigrated from a backstreet junk shop in Wolverhampton. Some of the juxtapositions verge on the crazy: a malachite Zulu head from South Africa next to a model of the American F111 fighter, which they gave me when I warned them that Britain would not be buying any. There are model soldiers and a dried starfish (a family proverb exists which accounts for the latter); and a china pink elephant given me in the middle of a political crisis by a daughter for consolation keeps company with a clockwork kangaroo and a pokerwork wooden plaque with my favourite text: 'The Lord will provide.'

In the middle of all this I work. Yes, I work; for if there is peace here, it is the peace of hard labour. A sanctum or snuggery the room decidedly is not; for this is the place where the work of life gets done – or that part of it which is not for doing in the Palace of Westminster. The worn desk (a Cambridge undergraduate's) and the office chair are surrounded by piles of working folders and loomed over by a lofty arrangement of filing trays, called the *ziggurat* from its resemblance to the towers of Babylon.

On reflection, what gives this room of mine its comforting and reassuring character is its very incongruity. The past years, unchangeable in their familiar shapes and now beyond the reach of effort or regret, observe with kindly tolerance the feverish endeavours crammed into the narrow space of the present, with a sort of Housmanic 'Lie down, lie down, young yeoman, The sun moves ever West.' The pokiness of the room – only a pace or two in any direction – is part of the secret of its soothing quality, as if the passion for concentration and self-sufficiency which is part of its occupant found a matching mood in the confined and crowded space. I think I never could be so at ease in a room with ample vistas and large acres of wall and carpet.

The same affinity for concentration makes it not only feasible but agreeable for the room to be in the middle of the busyness of the whole house: the doorbell, the voices and footsteps on the staircase, the telephone and its even more imperious companion, the 'intercom', are not banished from here. Let others build themselves summerhouses at the end of the garden or contrive sound-proof attics like Carlyle's in Cheyne Walk. They must be hypersensitive creatures, if they cannot hack their work out among the rough and tumble of the outer world.

What ought such a room, then, to be called? When those accustomed to the ways of the modern MP refer to it as my 'office', the sound is like scraping a knife on a saucepan. Yet something of an office, filing cabinets, typewriter, correspondence, it undeniably has. Nor again will 'study' do. The word is altogether too world-renouncing and world-shunning. Yet some of its contents are the materials of past, and indeed of present, study in the strict sense. 'Library' is not right either: a man can both transact business and study in his library, but 'library' implies something more spacious, more leisurely, an apartment with deep leather-upholstered chairs. So what is it in fact called? As long as there were children about the house, it was 'Daddy's room'. So now it has to be simply 'my room', no more or less than that.

JOHN RICHARDSON
NEW YORK

When, twenty-five years ago, I moved to New York to run Christies' US operation, I found myself faced with two floors of a seedy brownstone house to furnish 'on a shoe-string' and little idea of how to set about it. So far as decorating was concerned, I only had one hang-up: unlike many of my friends who prided themselves on their taste, I was in reaction against 'Fowlerism'. I was sick of the way house after house in England was falling victim to fashionable gentility. Austerely masculine rooms were being cosied up and prettified – too often emasculated in the process. A friend who should have known better had replaced library chairs in rusty morocco with a lot of buttoned love-seats and little lime green sofas; and wherever one looked canteloupe coloured cushions were making what decorators call 'statements' – rather shrill ones. The effect was as 'amusing' as a Nancy Mitford novel, and as arch and contrived as that lady's tinkling laugh. All the more genteel for endeavouring not to be! No, this pseudo-U look was all very well in SW7 but not at all suited to East 75th Street.

Imagine therefore my dismay when I discovered that the 'Fowlerism' I had fled in England was on the way to becoming the rage in New York. To judge by fashionable decorators, the cold, hard international style that had proved such a good match for the cold hard light and life-style of Manhattan was on the way out. A spurious English look – syntheticized beyond recognition – was on the way in. Rooms that had hitherto been keyed to an Eames chair, a rubber plant and a late Kandinsky were breaking out in a rash of 'Bailey Rose' ruffles, too much needlework and embroidered bellpulls that were only of service in so far as they gave a hint of height to very low rooms in very tall buildings. American friends assumed that, I, being English, would blindly follow this trend. They were wrong.

Instead I decided to have my apartment develop along aleatory lines. Rather than rush around trying

Right John Richardson in his room surrounded by what he calls his generous contributions. *Overleaf* The heraldic tapestry emblazoned with the red hand of Ulster guarded by a savage cheetah.

to match this with that, I took a leaf out of the Hippies' favourite book – remember it was the sixties – and consulted the *I Ching*. This enabled me to leave virtually everything to hazard: to scavenging, for example. I picked up lots of good stuff by patrolling the streets of the upper East Side on Wednesday evenings when insecurity gnaws at new rich matrons and they pile the sidewalks with cast-off furniture – anything that has lost its status or newness or chic. A borrowed station-wagon enabled me to load up the loot before the Salvation Army trucks did their nightly rounds, and many treasures I found.

Working for an auction house was also a help: I soon developed an instinct for the sleeper that lurks in every sale, and once in a while would acquire something good for a fraction of its worth. And then I was fortunate in having a number of generous friends who rallied round and made contributions – everything from a chipped Sèvres plate to a lethal toaster. Painters proved to be particularly charitable. Braque and Picasso had given me a number of drawings when I was living in France in the fifties. Now American artists turned out to be no less open-handed: Andy Warhol, Frank Stella and Robert Rauschenberg made major contributions to my walls. Ellsworth Kelly even frescoed the dining-room with monumental still lifes, but since these were executed in appropriate, if somewhat fugitive media – Worcester sauce, ketchup and Tabasco – they did not survive.

In no time the living-room filled up with such a heterogeneous accumulation of chattels that the question of decoration became moot. As I had hoped, the clash of disparate *trouvailles* gave my apartment its own special character. Nobody could accuse me of following this or that style or trend. In any case, most of my decisions were governed by financial considerations. If I settled for a set of rather grand brocade curtains from a house in Yorkshire, it was because I found them at Geoffrey Bennison's shop for less than a tenth of what my neighbourhood upholsterer had quoted for not very attractive ones. Atavism, too, played a role in the way things ultimately looked. If I opted for a chintz sofa, club fender or worn Turkey carpet, it was because such things reminded me of my Victorian father, not because these erstwhile staples of English sitting-rooms had been brought back into fashion by the popularity of British TV series. At one point the risk of being thought trendy tempted me to switch to G-Plan, but in the end I left things the way they were in the belief that the

English look would soon be overtaken by neo-this or post-that, and then my bits and pieces would once again be reassuringly 'out'. An important consideration this: on my side of the Atlantic people who make a point of keeping in step end up as clones.

Since I like things to be patinated by wear and tear and time, I have always tried to keep my rooms in a state of semi-shabbiness. Not all that difficult, given the presence of an accident-prone girl on the floor above. Unfortunately her ordeals by fire and water – ordeals I have been obliged to share – eventually pushed the process of patination beyond the limits of the picturesque. To camouflage water damage and exorcise sooty stains and smells and memories, I employed Malcolm Robson, an English grainer who has emigrated to Washington, to paint the damaged areas, some in imitation of grey and yellow marble, some in *bois clair* and mahogany – what a critical friend described as '*folie de grandeur* on the cheap'. 'Aren't the yellow marble walls a touch garish?' the same friend asked. The answer, of course, is yes, all that yellow cheers up what would otherwise be a gloomy little annexe to the living-room; it is also – here I look upwards and cross my fingers – a hostage to fate as well as to canons of fashionable taste.

Over the years I have come to see my New York apartment as a desperate rearguard action, a struggle against a magpie compulsion to accumulate fanciful junk. Every available penny goes on 'finds' which seldom serve any useful purpose: a giant tortoise (stuffed), a jester's rattle, a silver chamber-pot, daguerreotypes of circus freaks, a hunk of obsidian, several narwhal tusks, a gigantic coral brain, busts galore, an apron of giraffe tails, heraldic tapestries emblazoned with the red hand of Ulster and much, much more besides. 'The room represents the story of my life,' I feebly echo Mario Praz, and look round at the shambles and pray that it is nothing of the sort, that I am not that much of a mess.

At times, however, I love my over-cluttered room: when it smells of lilies in the summer, of woodsmoke in the winter, when the faint sounds of the city give way to the old-fashioned rattle of ice in a cocktail shaker, or the just audible *va-et-vient* of my dog. At moments like this its atmosphere seems, to me at least, palpably romantic. The only thing that manages to dissipate it is the telephone with its incessant demands and temptations. But it is as well to have a pretext for escaping from the unflattering narcissistic pool that one's surroundings threaten to become.

A.L.ROWSE

CORNWALL

The library at Trenarren House is a beautiful room, plain, late Georgian proportions, though added on about 1840 to the original Regency house, begun in the year of Trafalgar, 1805, a stone in the cellars tells us. In remote Cornwall one must allow for our being a generation or so behind London in architectural styles. So the room is essentially Georgian, with a wide southward window looking on to the terrace, then a steep lawn with rounded mound of rhododendrons at the bottom, thus down a magical valley and beyond – the sea.

Famous old Princess Bibesco, Proust's friend, used to detect an optical illusion – as if the sea, held in a V-shaped chalice, were above one's eye-level from outside on the terrace.

Within the room the Victorians did a thing or two typical of them. They left the decorative cornice that runs round the ceiling untouched, but they took away the surround of a dummy door placed symmetrically with the entrance door, and inserted china shelves. Opposite that they offended against symmetry again by inserting a westward-looking window, tall, Georgian proportions however.

Actually I am grateful for that. It brings in heavenly late afternoon light. While I work away at the table in the centre of the room, I look up to see marvellous effects of golden glow, or honey-coloured radiance coming through the screen of western trees. Or I am spied upon by an inquisitive robin from his perch in the escallonia at the corner. Other birds appear – thrushes and those we Cornish call 'greybirds', finches, tits, magpies and rooks descending from their rookery in the pines; best of all, pheasants in all their pride of colour. And in the severe January of 1985, a long-beaked snipe and a couple of crested plover from the high moors inland.

Nothing of all this distracts me from the work in hand. I find it refreshing to look up now and again at the glorious colours of the rare rhododendrons and camellias in the spring, the purple of ponticums coming on later in May and June. I often register 'How beautiful! how incredibly lovely!' and back to my task again.

For the library is a good place for work – plenty of elbow room and space for books. In fact I was pushed out of the nice little house I formerly owned, simply by the growth of books. With a collection of some 10,000 I had to take on this country house belonging to an ancient West Country family. It has certainly proved propitious to work – as also did my rooms at All Souls.

How is it arranged for work?

First, the bookcases and shelves. Part of the design of the room were two splendid shallow alcoves filling the centre of two walls. A previous tenant had papered this over with a violent Reckitts-blue wallpaper. The first thing I did was to book that out, completely shelving the alcoves to obliterate the blue with hundreds of books – nothing more decorative.

Another horror this lady perpetrated was to take out the perfectly adequate Victorian marble mantelpiece – Jane Austen says 'mantelpiece', so why shouldn't I, in spite of Nancy Mitford? My predecessor, rather than precursor, then inserted an appalling long low fireplace etc. of raw rocks out of the Trenarren cliffs, sharp enough to cut your eye on the edge of them. And no idea of proportion, far too low and far too lengthy – just the sort of thing you see in lower-middle-class bijou residences. I fear the woman was a townee, no country lady.

Anyway, I couldn't bear the contraption. One day, on a visit to dear Agatha Christie and Max Mallowan at Wallingford, I spotted an exquisite Regency mantelpiece: white marble, small stags' heads sculpted at corners, pale rose inlay. On the shelf above, I placed a little marble bust of Wellington, a couple of bisque baskets (with clove-oranges for their scent), and a pair of small dark agate dishes.

The shelves that occupied the dummy door opposite the western window I filled with my collection of Chinese blue-and-white porcelain – nothing very grand, but a pretty and colourful variation on the massed books. And some Chinese ivory miniatures – brought home in my socks from San Diego – to variegate the china.

Beside that stands a modest white bookcase that contains mostly Shakespeare and the Elizabethan dramatists, conveniently together. For there is roughly a plan of various sections, different subjects, that the library contains – though by no means the whole of my books. At least half-a-dozen more rooms, besides the corridors, are filled with books, different rooms and areas covering different subjects.

I think of the library as my main research-and-writing place, devoted to research books I am writing on the Tudor and Stuart periods, Elizabethan, Shakespeare and the Civil War. (Autobiographical and Cornish books I write in an upstairs study where the relevant material is – books, diaries, journals, manuscripts. Poetry I confine to my bedroom.)

In the big alcoves one section concentrates on Tudor history, another on Elizabethan history and literature; a third makes a sixteenth-century foreign and Renaissance section, a fourth has art-history books covering that period at home and abroad (a bigger and more general collection in an upstairs corridor). Some shelves have pure research material for my chosen period: Calendars of State Papers, Acts of the Privy Council, volumes of the Historical Mss. Commission, the vast *New English Dictionary* and the latest edition of the *Encyclopaedia Britannica*. (More research material fills both my downstairs study and a third upstairs study.)

It will be seen that even in the library there is something to go on with; and I go on with it at a big early Victorian breakfast table (date of the room) always littered with papers and manuscripts, for I write everything longhand. If I could only type, it would treble my inadequate rate of production.

One more bookcase: a fine stout glass-fronted reproduction of Georgian type, mahogany like all the furniture, with roomy cupboards: locked, for this contains rare books of the periods I am interested in. On top, two fine big vases of Mason's Chinese ironstone, of the exact date of the house. Beside it, a voluptuously carved and sculpted stand with shell on top – I forget what you call it – which will hold a large bowl of flowers from the garden to enliven that corner.

In front of the big window is a big serpentine-fronted Georgian writing desk, again covered with papers and manuscripts. It and the drawers on either side are dedicated mainly to Shakespeare. I find it a great help to concentration to stick to a certain division of labour for work – answering letters and chores, paying bills etc., in the downstairs study.

Pictures, not many to distract attention. Over the fireplace a Georgian portrait of one Hudson, of a family of eighteenth-century Oxford musicians: quite good, but the decorative gilt frame even better – I bought it for the frame. A seventeenth-century portrait is rather a mystery, unknown, no identification. It is of a scholar, chaste black coat and white collar, and with a scholar's motto: Magis Amica Veritas, a phrase from the famous tag, Plato is a friend, Aristotle too, but a greater friend is Truth. It depicts well a fine open face, that looks to me like the engraving of the great John Selden. The portrait has no coat of arms, which makes me think so even more, for Selden was not armigerous.

Two landscapes come from my collecting in the 1930s: a Cornish landscape by Christopher Wood, very characteristic and one of his best; and a charming Céria of Sanary – a distinguished painter not so well known: I bought it in London long ago because it reminded me nostalgically of Looe.

I bought an old Aubusson specially for this room, along with three lovely French needlework rugs. Two bigger ones I got when hardly more than a boy at Oxford: a Bokhara of rare colouring, fawn with pattern in indigo blue, and a gay peach-coloured Susak.

Altogether the library has the right atmosphere for work: peaceful and secluded, no telephone, nothing to distract or offend, nothing ghostly – as in the upstairs corridors, where I sometimes fancy I hear the swish-oo of a Victorian lady's skirt, vanishing round the corner. There was a Victorian lady-writer, Gertrude Parsons, née Hext, who lived in the house and wrote improving novels for maidservants. Though not quite up to that, I think of myself as her successor; no doubt she would think me a dull dog, tied to table or desk scribble-scribble-scribble at historical or literary research.

Previous page Some of Dr Rowse's 10,000 books are housed
in convenient alcoves.
Above A bust of Wellington on the mantelpiece.

GAVIN STAMP

LONDON

I have a Victorian print entitled 'My Den'. It shows a shabby, bookish old gent seated at a chaotic desk. He is reading a book in a room piled high with books and papers. This is not an ideal to which I aspire but a reality I unfailingly succeed in achieving. Any room I inhabit is a mess. I am untidy, disorganized and chaotic and I create a muddle of piles of books, piles of paper and books open for reference all around me. Sometimes, very occasionally, I try to control the muddle and tidy up, but things soon revert to normal. My room is a hopeless machine for working in.

As well as being untidy I am incapable of finishing anything. This room has bare plaster walls and stripped, singed woodwork. I always have elaborate, wonderful plans for decoration but they are never brought to a successful conclusion. After the initial enthusiasm wears off, I become used to disorder and rawness. Soon one simply does not notice any more. When I lived in a bachelor flat in an Edwardian vicarage in south London, I planned an authentic colour scheme in dark, properly old-fashioned colours. But somehow the stencilled frieze I started never circumnavigated the room, and the intended effect was soon impeded and overwhelmed by the constantly growing piles of books and papers as well as the absurd profusion of propped-up postcards, invitations and other cherished and contrived ephemera. As well as being disorganized, I am too whimsical and accumulative to live up to the precious ideals of interior decorators. But what true Englishman's room does?

Marriage has not helped. I do not mean that my wife is quite as chaotic and untidy as I am; it is just that she has not attempted to reform me as she is not capable of being orderly herself (she did, after all, invent the appalling artistic 'Filth-Packets' family for *Harpers & Queen* magazine). She is, however, full of decorative schemes of her own. As these change every week, it is probably a good thing that the house remains unfinished. I cannot think why some people

are so keen to 'do up' houses. It is a long, laborious process which requires careful thought. Old houses deserve to be restored slowly and carefully.

Three years ago we bought this standard Late Georgian Fourth Rate London terraced house, built the year Beethoven died according to the *Survey of London* (I mean to look up the old rate books and deeds, but, of course, I have not got round to that either). It is in King's Cross, and out of the back upstairs windows we can see the clock towers of both St Pancras and King's Cross stations (usually showing different times): so convenient for travelling to Edinburgh, Luton or Stevenage. I have always wanted to live in central London and have twice succeeded in living near main-line railway termini. I do not wish to be in the country or in a suburb and cannot comprehend why fools pay a fortune to live in western deserts like Fulham.

This three-storey house was once a sleazy lodging house – or worse, for this area used to be better known for red lights than for elegant façades. This was fortunate, and not only because the house was cheap. In smart parts of London, houses have been modernized and restored over and over again, so that practically nothing original is left. Here, the chimneypieces had gone but everything else – doors, staircase, cornices, etc. – had survived, albeit punctuated by tiresome holes for Yale locks or for the water and waste pipes which serviced the basins which once graced every single room.

The fireplaces we put back straight away: no room is complete without a chimneypiece. Here, on the first floor, we have the proper *piano nobile* with two rooms connected by the original double doors. The back drawing room now has a fine reeded marble chimneypiece of authentic date which was a wedding present from the Fitzalan Pursuivant Extraordinary, that is, the architectural historian John Martin Robinson (two chimneypieces from Dan Cruickshank are elsewhere in the house). This is filled by an antique 1920s gas fire which, I hope, looks as if it has always been there. In fact, it was supplied by Charles Brooking, the architectural salvage fanatic. One of my many complaints against the modern world is that new gas fires will not fit into existing old grates and look hideous. The horrible Gas Board seem determined to do away both with old gas fires and old fireplaces.

The principal chimneypiece in the front drawing-

room we actually bought. The marble surround is a little late in date for the house, though, in fact, much of the internal joinery also seems to be Victorian. Here, in a neo-classical grate cast by the famous Carron works, we burn coal. I have no moral objection to the new gas coal fires with real flames which clean-minded aesthetes install, but I prefer real coal (Coalite, theoretically, to comply with the Clean Air Act) and, besides, we have a coal cellar complete with a coal hole in the pavement. I think the coal merchant rather enjoys pouring the sack loads through it rather than humping it all through the house.

The coal also contributes an important element to the character of the room, as it is responsible for a fine layer of ash everywhere. All horizontal surfaces are coated in a rich deposit of dust which is many months thick. Dust, it seems to me, is an integral part of the Englishman's room. There seems no point in cleaning it off when it only accumulates again and, besides, it is impossible to clean around piles of paper, books and cards. Unfortunately, however, the dust is at present augmented by cigarette ash, which I do not find at all romantic. My wife, being female, smokes when I am not around. She really ought to be out working but, at present, she is at home writing a book. The result is that she muddles up the back drawing-room with paper and has an antique Imperial typewriter balanced on the piano stool (her piano: I cannot play) while I have my Corona portable (c. 1925) and my own muddle in the front drawing-room. At the moment, therefore, there is twice the amount of chaos. It is absolute hell, especially as our small daughter greatly enjoys knocking over piles of notes and tearing up paper.

Although fitted up with chandeliers and furnished with Indian rugs, the two drawing-rooms remain undecorated. On moving in, the first thing we did, after throwing out piles of slug-ridden mattresses, was to hire a 'steam stripper' and get layers of paper off the walls. This had a curious side effect. The steam fug condensed on the ceiling and mixed with the rich deposit of cigarette smoke to drip on our bare shoulders as liquid nicotine. Revolting, especially as I do not need anti-smoking therapy. Fortunately the plaster is in good condition although, in places, we could not get off a layer of paint. Friends with old-fashioned Modern tastes say: leave it. Don't touch a thing! I fear they mean it. I am longing to put up wallpaper but our energies at first went into

Previous page Long late-Georgian windows with
curtains of unbleached calico. Chairs serve as filing
cabinets while the perplexed owner surveys the chaos.

The front drawing-room fireplace. Here the walls
of bare plaster are anything but bare of architectural
pictures.

decorating the bedrooms and the kitchen in the basement. Also, we cannot agree on what wallpaper to have. I suppose I can imagine the buff cracked plaster looking rather Palladian and chic. Indeed, to get a clever stainer and grainer to achieve this decaying *palazzo* effect would be very expensive. As it is, it is very economical, as is the treatment of the joinery. The Bloomsbury mottled finish is achieved by the inept use of a blow-lamp.

The curtains are also very economical, being made of unbleached calico normally used for stage sets. They hang well and look suitably Regency even if they are utterly useless at keeping out light and keeping in heat. Unfortunately, they really will have to go as I recently noticed a fashionable interior decorator recommending unbleached calico curtains. I *loathe* interior decorators and cannot understand why anyone with a modicum of sense and style would ever employ one.

As for the furniture, it is a mixture of aspiring antiques and pieces of utilitarian junk which I long to replace. The important thing is that tables should be able to bear the weight of piles of books and that chairs should perform as filing cabinets. One cabinet conceals the gramophone and radio – permanently tuned to the Third Programme. I don't think modern technology should be visible. Ideally, I would like the furniture to be of the date of the house because, more and more, the first few decades of the nineteenth century seem to me to be a high point in civilization. Unfortunately, rather too many other people feel the same. Try as we will, we are all creatures of fashion and prisoners of the *Zeitgeist*. Some of the better pieces come from antique shops, but the Biedermeier sofa and several of the chairs came from Brick Lane for a song. They are all broken, with wobbly legs, but I never mind that. The cat also contributes to their mellow, time-worn, authentic appearance; she has sharp claws.

The walls may be of bare plaster but they are not bare. I cannot abide rooms without pictures and, ideally, I would like them from floor to ceiling. There cannot be too many. I have absolutely no sympathy for that austere, puritanical, joyless approach which demands no clutter and just a few choice objects in a room of awful, boring whiteness. Such rooms are not for real, clumsy human beings. I would rather have lots of moderately good things than one exceptional object. I fear I love possessions: no doubt it is a vice. I cannot stop buying more prints or more second-hand books. As regards the pictures, I like anything, providing it is of a building. All the pictures in this room are architectural, the subjects ranging from Ely Cathedral to the Woolworth skyscraper in New York. There are a few Piranesis, a Daniel and some proof Pugin prints of the Brighton Pavilion. Nothing is that special; the best is the watercolour perspective of St Pancras New Church, in the parish of which we live. I would like more original architectural drawings but they, alas – like so much I admire – have become so fearfully expensive and beyond my means.

Finally, over the carpets, furniture, mantelpieces and shelves, there is the essential profusion of accumulated clutter. There are piles of newspapers, piles of *Spectators*, piles of *Private Eyes*; there are postcards, ancient invitations, dirty glasses, coins, prints, photographs and a truly distressing number of empty whisky bottles lying all over the place. It is so very difficult to throw anything away. On top of the piano I fear there is not only a pile of last year's Christmas cards but the collection for 1983 as well.

I am describing this as my room but, of course, it is not. I have to share it with others; it is, after all, a drawing-room and my working in it is tolerated as a temporary arrangement. We have a great Ten Year Plan. The ground floor, which is at present uninhabited and occupied entirely by bicycles, prams, cat litter trays and huge collapsing piles of books, is intended to house a proper dining-room and a library, lined with shelves, for me to work in. But somehow I suspect that this will never happen.

A miscellany of treasures on the chimneypiece.

DAVID SYLVESTER

LONDON

The room is in a rented flat on the ground floor of a four-storey house in south London built in the 1860s and converted in the 1950s. The flat consists of the rump of an entrance hall, a bathroom inserted into the space under the stairs, a kitchen set up in a corridor to the garden, and three rooms that were built as rooms. Each of them has a dual purpose now. The one at the front is for writing and occasionally for eating; the smaller room at the back is a library and a lumber room, the larger a bed-sitting-room. To write about the things in that last room and how they came to be arranged as they are first requires, I'm afraid, a digression into some personal history.

When I moved into the flat in 1959, it was with a wife and a baby daughter. Soon there were three daughters, and they had a disgracefully overcrowded upbringing, made even worse than it had to be by my putting the front room out of bounds. It was the room where grown-ups wined and dined, where I worked behind a sound-proofed door, where precious objects were secure. The initial precious objects were some splendid pieces of English furniture munificently passed on to us along with the flat by our friend John Hewett, the dealer in antiquities. Indeed, it was a desire to live with this furniture that had caused us to decline an alternative offer of a large flat close to the various furnished rooms we had had in SW1 and SW3 and to embark instead on our long migration across the Thames to SW18. Now, living with the furniture meant, of course, living up to the furniture. So my art collector's instinct started asserting itself irresistibly, spurred on by the generosity over prices of the same dealer friend. The objects became increasingly precious, the protective feeling about the room increasingly insistent, the preoccupation with achieving a perfect arrangement of its contents increasingly obsessive.

So the contrast grew between the serenity of that room and the sickening muddle of the rest. Then in 1967–8 I spent a year teaching at an American university, took the family with me and rented a house. For the first time in their lives the children had stairs to go up and down, and this made them feel – even more than it did to have rooms of their own – that at last they were living like human beings. Back in London, they repeatedly expressed a wish to go on doing so. I ignored this. For I had a fixation on large rooms like those of the flat, a fixation which made me insist that I couldn't buy a house until my parents died and left me with the money to buy one with large rooms. And then it occurred to me that, as the rent of the flat was low, I could afford both it and the purchase of a normal sort of house. In the summer of 1969 we moved into a very nice house in the neighbourhood while I kept on the flat for myself alone as a place for working, collecting art, and sometimes staying the night. By 1974 I was living there on my own – a fitting punishment and reward.

What I liked about taking the flat over for myself was that I now had two large rooms that could be beautiful; I resigned myself to making the third one purely practical. I decided that the large back room was to have a bed, an armchair, a chest and a lot of art – no wardrobe or chest of drawers (I kept my clothes in the library and the kitchen). I hung the walls with contemporary things, mostly American, all but one of them works on paper, by Barnett Newman, David Smith, Philip Guston, Jasper Johns and so forth; the other piece was an abstract sculpture in felt by Robert Morris, suspended from nine feet up, cascading thickly down the wall and spreading out in massive arabesques across the floor.

There were other wonders on the floor. At the time of buying the house I suddenly became aware that Islamic carpets existed which were at least as good to look at as abstract paintings that cost infinitely more. I had a suspicion that it would not be long before many other people awoke to this fact and that a price explosion would follow – I was right – so I started

buying them frantically, aiming to keep ahead of the market and continuously re-sell most of my acquisitions to improve the collection. Not surprisingly, the first thirty or so that I bought were of types whose colours and shapes are closest to twentieth-century Western painting – tribal and village rugs and kelims from Turkey and the Caucasus. And these are what went on the floor with the contemporary American art.

I liked the room and would have liked to leave it as it was. But I only had two rooms to play with, and the trouble was that I then made another discovery. After I had been looking at Islamic carpets for about a year I came to realize that what I had been collecting was kids' stuff by comparison with the classical carpets of the sixteenth, seventeenth and early eighteenth centuries. I also learned that it was possible to find marvellous examples of these at no great cost provided one didn't mind if the piece was a fragment or in poor condition or both. Personally I like the balance of the colour acquired by ancient carpets whose pile is low: the indigo tends to retain its density while the reds get a wonderful washed-out look. And carpet fragments have two great things to commend them. One is that they may be remnants of masterpieces of a class intact examples of which hardly exist outside museums. The other is that it suits fragments aesthetically to be hung on walls – whereas it does not really suit entire rugs – and this is convenient, since a wall is a practical location for old pieces, as they get to look even older if put on the floor and walked on.

It was the acquisition of a large fragment of an Indian palace carpet that made it necessary to transform the room. The fragment clearly had to fill the wall opposite the window. The pictures there had to go and so had the bed, which had been jutting out of that wall, and now had to replace the felt sculpture. As I was working hard at searching out pieces, it was not long before I found the other fragments and rugs which have stayed ever since on the walls and the bed. The moderns were gone. I now had to change the background. I had painted the walls a cool grey and the woodwork white; I changed both to a beige which I thought would mix with the carpets' shabby pinks and dirty gold and deep indigo. The difficult blend to achieve was with the carpet on the floor. It was always going to be an east Persian or Indian carpet, but three came and went over the years before I found the right one. The others were all better pieces, but they failed to harmonize precisely with those on the walls. The right one had in fact been shown to me by a dealer long before, newly imported from Italy: I had looked at it and asked him why he was bothering me with anything so third-rate. One day I saw it again in his shop and complained bitterly that he had never shown it to me before. He was merciful and charged only double his original price.

So I had a roomful of carpets now, faded old carpets, soft furnishings in nice contrast to the carvings in stone from Egypt and Greece and Rome in the next room. Only, these carvings had lately been joined by two African masks carved in wood – pieces which didn't fit in but which I had bought because they were too extraordinary not to buy. Howard Hodgkin, the painter, suggested that I should try them in the room with the carpets – a juxtaposition I had lacked the nerve to envisage. From then on I was adding African objects – masks, figures, stools, bowls, musical instruments, bronze bells. Many have come and gone; enough have stayed.

There was one thing I could not get right – the space over the fireplace, a fireplace that has a certain charm but is assertive as well as ugly. Over the years I tried old master paintings, modern paintings, drawings, prints, carpet fragments, silk textiles, masks and a blank wall behind sculptures or objects on the shelf. About two years ago I suddenly found an object that seemed to work there, a musical instrument called a harp-lute, made in London around 1790. It probably fits because of its play between symmetry and asymmetry and because it's a sort of mask that has no face.

Previous page The author 'living up to the furniture'.
Left Fragments of Indian carpets hang on a beige wall, and an oriental carpet covers the floor.

BIOGRAPHICAL NOTES

SIR HAROLD ACTON

Harold Acton was born in 1904 in Florence, where he still resides. After his education at Eton and Christ Church, Oxford, he spent seven happy years in Peking where he collaborated in translations of modern Chinese poems and classical plays and taught English literature at Peking National University. During the Second World War he served in the RAF as an Intelligence and Public Relations officer. His most familiar writings are historical: *The Last Medici, The Bourbons of Naples, The Last Bourbons of Naples, Tuscan Villas,* etc. He has also published poems, novels, short stories, two volumes of memoirs, and a memoir of Nancy Mitford.

HARDY AMIES

In the 1930s Hardy Amies rose to become one of Britain's leading couturiers, and his salon is one of the few left in this country to rival the great dress houses of Paris. For over thirty years he has been dressmaker to the Queen. During the war he left the world of couture to serve as an Intelligence officer in the SOE. His favourite pastime is gardening at his Oxfordshire home.

QUENTIN BELL

Quentin Bell, the son of Vanessa and Clive Bell, was born in 1910 in Bloomsbury and educated as an artist (his academic decorations may be considered purely cosmetic). During the war he worked in Political Warfare Executive, and afterwards taught at several universities. He has written a life of Virginia Woolf and other books, his latest being a novel. He is now a potter and sculptor.

SIMON BLOW

Simon Blow left school at sixteen to work in racing stables at Newmarket. Following that, he worked in publishing in London and Paris. He gave up publishing for writing, and since then his work has appeared in many publications. His first book, *Fields Elysian: a portrait of hunting society*, was published in 1983. He is currently writing the story of his grandmother's family, the Tennants, which is to be published by Faber & Faber. He lives in London.

DIRK BOGARDE

Since 1947 Dirk Bogarde has starred in more than sixty films. His popularity as a teenage idol brought him vast amounts of fanmail and an enormous box-office success, which was to continue through the fifties and sixties. Later he achieved a different kind of success with such films as *The Servant, King and Country, Accident, Death in Venice, The Night Porter, Providence* and *Despair.* In recent years he has become well known as a writer with the publication of three volumes of autobiography and two novels. For the last fourteen years he has lived in Provence and was made a Chevalier de l'Ordre des Arts et des Lettres by the French Government in 1982, and an honorary Doctor of Letters at St Andrews University.

RICHARD BUCKLE

Richard Buckle was born in 1916 and was educated at Marlborough and Balliol. He then joined the Scots Guards from 1940 to 1946. He was the ballet critic of the *Observer* from 1948 to 1955 and of the *Sunday Times* from 1959 to 1975. Among the exhibitions he has organized are the Diaghilev Exhibition (1954–5), the Epstein Memorial Exhibition at the Edinburgh Festival (1961), the Shakespeare Exhibition, Stratford-on-Avon (1964), and the Beaton Portraits Exhibition, National Portrait Gallery (1968). He is the author of biographies of Nijinsky and Diaghilev, and has written many other books. He was instrumental in founding the Theatre Museum, and was awarded the CBE in 1979.

QUENTIN CREWE

Quentin Crewe has been a journalist, a farmer and a restaurateur. He has also written several travel books, in particular an account of a two-year journey through the Sahara. His most recent book is a biography of the last Maharaja of Jaipur. He is at present working on a book about the Caribbean. He has been married more than once and has five children.

THE DUKE OF DEVONSHIRE

The Duke of Devonshire was born in 1920 and educated at Eton and Cambridge. He joined the Coldstream Guards in 1940, serving until 1946. He stood as Conservative candidate for Chesterfield in 1945 and again in 1950, when he succeeded his father as 11th Duke. In 1960 he was appointed Parliamentary Under-Secretary of State at the Colonial Office, becoming Minister of State from 1962 to 1964. He was Steward of the Jockey Club from 1967 to

1970. He has concerned himself with a number of national charities. The Duke has been Chancellor of Manchester University since 1966, and was made a member of the Privy Council in 1964. He has lived at Chatsworth since 1959 and has one son and two daughters.

CHRISTOPHER GIBBS
Christopher Gibbs was born in 1938 and has been lucky enough to live in lovely places, chiefly in England, and to have known people who early in life introduced him to natural wonders, to history, art and architecture. After Eton and Paris and travels in the Holy Land, he began to deal in beautiful things and has spent his life trying to pass on to others something of what he has learned to love and take delight in.

SIR JOHN GIELGUD
Sir John Gielgud was born in 1904 and made his first appearance on the stage in 1921. Throughout his life he has been a leading actor in Shakespearean and other classical parts on the stage and in films, but he has also appeared in more popular roles and was awarded an Oscar in 1982 for his performance in *Arthur*. He is the author of *An Actor and his Time*, published in 1979.

THE EARL OF HAREWOOD
George Lascelles, Earl of Harewood, son of the 6th Earl of Harewood and HRH Princess Mary, was born in 1923. He served in the Grenadier Guards during the war, and thereafter has worked in musical administration. He was founder and editor of *Opera* magazine, editor and reviser of Kobbé's *Complete Opera Book*, Opera Planner at Covent Garden, Artistic Director of the Leeds and Edinburgh Festivals, and chairman of many committees. He retired in 1985 after thirteen years as Managing Director of the English National Opera.

JOHN HARRIS
John Harris is the Curator of the Drawings Collection and Heinz Gallery in Portman Square. Although an historian of architecture and gardening, he has many 'secret orchards', not the least being chairman of the oldest firm of art dealers in the world, and an authority on the literary expression of the First World War. He writes much, but has always regretted not being a tank commander, preferably of the Patton mould.

SIR NICHOLAS HENDERSON
Sir Nicholas Henderson, the son of Professor Sir Hubert Henderson, was in the diplomatic service as Minister to Madrid and Ambassador to Warsaw, Bonn, Paris, and Washington. He has published several books, including *Prince Eugen of Savoy*, *The Birth of NATO*, *The Private*

Office, and stories and articles in numerous publications. He is a director of various companies, a member of the Council of the Duchy of Cornwall, chairman of the Channel Tunnel Group, a trustee of the National Gallery, an Honorary Fellow of Hertford College, Oxford, and President of the Hartford Society. For long an active yet absentee gardener, he is now a present but less active participant.

THE HON. DAVID HERBERT
David Herbert has always enjoyed life. He liked school – for the companionship not for the work – then at a fairly early age became the renegade of the family. He went to Berlin and sang in a night club before the advent of Hitler; then he ran away to America, was cut off by the family, worked in an antiques business, came home and acted in films directed by Elinor Glyn. He joined the Merchant Navy during the war, and emigrated to Morocco in 1947. His autobiography, *Second Son*, emphasized what fun it was to be one as it involved no responsibility. He settled down happily in Tangier, in a house and garden he loves, looked after by devoted staff and surrounded by pets of all descriptions.

DAVID HICKS
David Hicks was born in 1929. He was educated at Charterhouse and the London School of Arts and Crafts and served in the Royal Army Education Corps for two and a half years. He started decorating in 1954. His Brussels weave carpet collection and his collection of furnishing fabrics and wallpapers were said to 'have caused the geometric revolution in America'. 101 Jermyn Street, London, is the headquarters of David Hicks International. He has published eight books on design and decoration for houses and gardens, and has been employed by countless famous people all over the world. He is married to the former Lady Pamela Mountbatten.

MILES HILDYARD
Miles Hildyard was born in 1914. His father, a KC, inherited Flintham Hall. He was educated at Eton. In 1939 he went to Palestine with the Yeomanry. He was captured in Crete, escaped to Greece and Turkey, and rejoined his regiment for Alamein and the Western Desert. He served as an Intelligence officer in the 7th armoured division, and was awarded the MC and MBE. After the war he was called to the Bar but took over the family farm. He is interested in conservation and has been vice-chairman and chairman of the Notts Branch of the Council for the Preservation of Rural England for thirty years. He is vice-chairman of the National Trust, East Midlands, President of the Thoroton Society (local history and archaeology), and FSA (Fellow of the Society of Antiquaries). He is a keen gardener and tree planter, DL and JP. He is not married.

DEREK HILL

Derek Hill was born in 1916. He is a painter of landscapes and portraits, a traveller and a writer. He has had two books published by Faber & Faber on *Islamic Architectural Decoration* and a third is in progress. He started as a stage designer, learning in Munich, Vienna and Moscow, and designed sets for *Il Trovatore* at Covent Garden, and a Frederick Ashton ballet at Sadler's Wells. He has painted portraits of HRH the Prince of Wales, Sir Isaiah Berlin, Bernard Berenson, Sir Michael Tippett, Arthur Rubinstein, Sir Yehudi Menuhin, etc., and his works are in the Tate Gallery, the National Gallery of Canada, the National Gallery of Ireland, the National Portrait Gallery, the Scottish Gallery of Modern Art, etc. He has lived in Ireland for over thirty years.

GERVASE JACKSON-STOPS

Gervase Jackson-Stops was educated at Harrow and Christ Church, Oxford, and subsequently held a Museums Association Award at the Victoria and Albert Museum from 1969 to 1972. Since then he has held the post of Architectural Adviser to the National Trust, and has also been a regular contributor to *Country Life* since 1972, writing on art and architectural history. He has recently organized the major exhibition of *The Treasure Houses of Britain* at the National Gallery, Washington DC, and has collaborated with the American photographer James Pipkin on a book, *The English Country House – A Grand Tour*.

THE VISCOUNT LAMBTON

Antony Lambton was born in 1922 and educated at Harrow and Sandhurst. During the Second World War he served in the Hampshire Regiment. In 1951, as Lord Lambton, he was elected Conservative Member for Berwick-on-Tweed. He resigned from Parliament in 1973, since when he has lived mostly in Italy and has contributed to several national newspapers. He has recently had published *Elizabeth and Alexandra*, a biography of the daughters of the Grand Duke of Hesse.

JAMES LEES-MILNE

James Lees-Milne was born and brought up in a Worcestershire manor house. On leaving Oxford University he worked for four years as private secretary to the proconsul, Lord Lloyd of Dolobran. From 1936 to 1966 he was in charge of the National Trust's historic houses and their collections. He has written some twenty-five books on architectural subjects, several diaries, biographies and two novels. He is married to Alvilde Lees-Milne.

PATRICK LEIGH FERMOR

Patrick Leigh Fermor was born in 1915. After a calamitous school career and a year-and-a-half journey on foot to Constantinople, he lived and travelled in the Balkans and the Greek Archipelago. During that time he acquired a deep interest in languages and a love of remote places. He joined the Irish Guards in 1939, and fought in Greece and Crete to which, during the German occupation, he returned three times (once by parachute). Disguised as a shepherd, he lived for over two years in the mountains organizing the resistance and the capture and evacuation of the German Commander, General Kreipe. He was awarded the DSO in 1944 and the OBE in 1943. Patrick Leigh Fermor's books include *The Traveller's Tree*, about the West Indies, which won the Heinemann Foundation Prize for Literature in 1950; *A Time of Gifts*, winner of the 1978 W. H. Smith & Son Annual Literary Award; and *Mani*, which won the Duff Cooper Memorial Prize. He has designed and built a house in Greece, where he now lives.

EDWARD MILLINGTON-DRAKE

Edward Millington-Drake was born in 1932 in London and spent his childhood in Uruguay where his father was British Minister. He came to school in England at the age of ten, and later went to live in Paris to study painting. Since then he has lived in Italy and in Greece and since 1973 has had a house near Siena. His first three exhibitions were of drawings and watercolours. Then for fifteen years he was a non-figurative painter. He returned to figurative painting in India and has exhibited regularly in that style – mostly watercolours of India, which he visited every year for many years.

DAVID MLINARIC

David Mlinaric has been working as an interior designer and decorator in London for twenty-three years. His work has nearly always been in old buildings and in a traditional style, and he is particularly interested in the problem of adjusting an old building to a new purpose. Most of his work has been in private houses, but he has worked in public buildings, hotels and restaurants, houses for the National Trust and embassies abroad. He thinks that, at its best, the English way of arranging houses and then living in them is the most satisfactory to be found in the western world. His view is that rooms are for living in first, and looking at second.

PROFESSOR BERNARD NEVILL

Bernard Nevill is Professor of Textiles at the Royal College of Art. He was designer and design director for Liberty prints from 1960 to 1970. His internationally acclaimed Jazz, Tango print collections were the first to revive and re-appraise art deco, and together with his subsequent work were instrumental in re-establishing Liberty's as a major fabric source for leading designers and fashion houses worldwide. His current work includes the English

Gardens and Botanic collections for Romanex de Boussac, France. An ardent conservationist and environmentalist, he has been engaged for the past eight years in the reconstruction of the remaining wing of Fonthill Abbey and in the restoration and landscaping of its gardens and woodlands.

NIGEL NICOLSON

Nigel Nicolson, the son of Harold Nicolson and Vita Sackville-West, is an author and publisher. Having co-founded the firm of Weidenfeld & Nicolson in 1948, he was for seven years a Member of Parliament. He now lives at Sissinghurst Castle in Kent. Among his books are *Portrait of a Marriage* (a study of his parents) and most recently an account of Napoleon's Russian campaign in 1812.

TOM PARR

Tom Parr started his career as an antique dealer, in which role he joined David Hicks in 1956 to form Hicks & Parr. In 1960 he joined Colefax & Fowler where, while looking after the Antiques Department, as he still does, he became more and more interested in the decorating side and has been actively involved in decorating ever since. He became senior partner on John Fowler's retirement. He now spends his time between London and his house in the South of France. He is doing virtually no decorating but has remained as chairman of the company.

THE RT HON. J. ENOCH POWELL, MP

Enoch Powell was born in 1912 and became a Fellow of Trinity College, Cambridge, in 1934. From 1937 to 1939 he was Professor of Greek at the University of Sydney, New South Wales, Australia. He joined the army as a private soldier in 1939 and rose to be a lieutenant-colonel in 1947. He has been Member of Parliament for County Down, Northern Ireland, since 1974, and was Minister for Health from 1960 to 1963. He has published several volumes of verse in translation from the Greek, and his numerous books include *The Life of Joseph Chamberlain*, published in 1977, as well as political pamphlets.

JOHN RICHARDSON

Author of books on Manet, Braque and Picasso and formerly head of Christie's US operations, John Richardson is a British art historian who has lived in New York and Connecticut for most of the last twenty-five years. In addition to being Consulting Editor of American *House & Garden*, he is currently writing a biography of Pablo Picasso.

A. L. ROWSE

Born in 1903 in Cornwall, A. L. Rowse was educated at the local grammar school and then at Christ Church, Oxford, as a scholar. He is an Emeritus Fellow of All Souls College, Oxford, and has spent most of his life researching into, and writing about, the Elizabethan age and its greatest writer, William Shakespeare. In this he has found it a great advantage to be a poet as well as a historian. Poetry came first, and he has written poetry all his life; the poetry expressing his inner life, the history the outer. He has retired now to his native parish, on the coast of Cornwall, with regular visits to Oxford and the USA.

GAVIN STAMP

In Gavin Stamp's passport his profession is grandly given as 'architectural historian', but that is because in many countries he would be even less welcome as a mere 'journalist'. In Britain, where he is the architectural correspondent of the *Spectator*, he is loathed by most modern architects and much of his writing is anonymous, for good reason. He is also chairman of the Thirties Society, dedicated to the preservation of Sir Giles Scott's beautiful telephone kiosks. With his wife, Alexandra Artley, and daughter and cat, he lives near a London main-line railway terminus. In 1984 Viking published his book *The Changing Metropolis* to great acclaim.

DAVID SYLVESTER

David Sylvester was born in 1924 in London and has spent most of his life there. His work has been concerned mainly with modern art, primarily through writing and talking about it but also through selecting and installing exhibitions, making films, interviewing and editing (and sitting on various committees). He is currently working on the catalogue raisonné of René Magritte, on a new edition of the book, *Interviews with Francis Bacon*, and on an exhibition of late Picasso for the Tate Gallery and the Musée National d'Art Moderne.